Mags Duggan

GOD
AMONG THE
RUINS

BRF

For Jenny

God among the Ruins

The Bible Reading Fellowship
15 The Chambers, Vineyard
Abingdon OX14 3FE
brf.org.uk

The Bible Reading Fellowship (BRF) is a Registered Charity (233280)

ISBN 978 0 85746 575 5
First published 2018
10 9 8 7 6 5 4 3 2 1 0
All rights reserved

Text © Mags Duggan 2018
This edition © The Bible Reading Fellowship 2018
Cover image © Thinkstock

Acknowledgements
Unless otherwise acknowledged, scripture quotations from the Holy Bible, New Living
Translation, copyright © 1996, 2004, 2007, 2013. Used by permission of Tyndale House
Publishers, Inc., Carol Stream, Illinois 60188. All rights reserved. • Scripture quotations
taken from The Holy Bible, New International Version (Anglicised edition) copyright
© 1979, 1984, 2011 by Biblica. Used by permission of Hodder & Stoughton Publishers,
a Hachette UK company. All rights reserved. 'NIV' is a registered trademark of Biblica.
UK trademark number 1448790. • Scripture quotations taken from the American
Standard Version of the Bible (public domain). • Scripture taken from THE MESSAGE.
Copyright © 1993, 1994, 1995, 1996, 2000, 2001, 2002. Used by permission of NavPress
Publishing Group. • Scripture quotations taken from the Amplified® Bible. Copyright ©
1954, 1958, 1962, 1964, 1965, 1987 by The Lockman Foundation. Used by permission.
(www.Lockman.org) • Scripture quotations from The New Revised Standard Version
of the Bible, Anglicised edition, copyright © 1989, 1995 by the Division of Christian
Education of the National Council of the Churches of Christ in the United States of
America. Used by permission. All rights reserved. • Scripture quotations from the
Contemporary English Version. New Testament © American Bible Society 1991,
1992, 1995. Old Testament © American Bible Society 1995. Anglicisations © British
& Foreign Bible Society 1996. Used by permission. • *The New Testament in Modern
English*, Revised Edition, translated by J.B. Phillips, published by HarperCollins
Publishers Ltd. Copyright © 1958, 1960, 1972 by J.B. Phillips. • Poem on p. 49 taken
from *When Life Takes What Matters* © 1993 by Susan Lenzkes. Used by permission of
Discovery House Publishers, Box 3566, Grand Rapids MI 4950l. All rights reserved.

Every effort has been made to trace and contact copyright owners for material used
in this resource. We apologise for any inadvertent omissions or errors, and would
ask those concerned to contact us so that full acknowledgement can be made in
the future.

A catalogue record for this book is available from the British Library

Printed and bound by CPI Group (UK) Ltd, Croydon CR0 4YY

Contents

Acknowledgements

I am so grateful for the faithful companions who walked with me through the circumstances which springboarded this book into being, and for those who continued to walk with me through the writing of the book itself.

Without the friendship, encouragement and initiative of Tony Horsfall, this book would not be in print. Thank you, Tony, for believing that the content of this book was worth sharing, for the confidence you inspired in me that I could actually write it and for writing a Foreword that reduced me to tears!

I was gifted with the kindest and wisest of editors in Mike Parsons at BRF, whose light touch gently shaped my writing when I so needed it. Thank you, Mike, for your constant encouragement and for your faith in this book; I feel deeply privileged that you took the risk of taking me on and guiding me so well.

This book has been birthed and nurtured in prayer, and I want to thank the many who prayed for me through the writing and shaping of the book. In particular, I want to thank those who have been my 'Moments with Mags' prayer partners over the years. Your prayers held me and undergirded me not just through the writing of this book, but through all the circumstances that led up to it. Thank you for such faithfulness. Special thanks, too, for the 'life support' involvement of Colin and Ann, Rob and Susie, Diane and Jo and Michael, Emma-Louise and David, and Keith and Wendy. Thank you for all the ways that you have been there for me these past years; for caring for me and my questions and wonderings. Thank you for the space and time you have given so generously.

King David had his 'mighty men' around him, who supported and strengthened him with their presence and their faithful commitment when he embarked on any new initiative. I have been blessed to have my own band of 'mighty men and women' in this venture – friends who kept praying for me, kept checking on me, kept cheering me on. For Pauline, Tracy, Shelley, Di, Rosemary, Pippa, MaryKate and Karen K. – thanks, you amazing women, that even in the midst of your own demanding lives, you somehow created the time to communicate, to provoke my thinking, to listen. This book is richer because of your influence. Thanks too to Dave A., Debs A.S., Rachael W., David and Anne, Ed and Conni, Ruth and Rich, Tom and Lis, Craig and Kris, John and Jen, Jonathan and Jessica, and unnamed, but beloved friends on the EA team (you know who you are). Your steady care and prayers are woven into the very fabric of this book and, more, into my life. Thank you so much.

I want to acknowledge my sister Keziah, whose quiet dignity, strength and courage through the most heartbreaking of circumstances has been truly inspiring; I admire you more than I can say, and love you more. And my mum, Mary, whose steady presence has been a constant through all the awfulness of the trauma we've been through as a family. Thanks for always being there, dear Mum, and for loving us so well and so wisely. Love you too.

And finally, my thanks to my dear friend Karen Anderson, who read every word of every sentence, however many times I rewrote them; who prayed over every word I wrote, and who kept encouraging me when I didn't think I could write another word. Karen, you always believed I could do this, and there would be no book without your support and your faith in God for me. Thank you, from my heart, for everything.

Foreword

Mags Duggan is a close friend for whom I have the upmost regard. Warm-hearted and humorous, Mags is a gifted speaker but also a wise listener. She has had a lifetime of serving God as a missionary with the Navigators and, most recently, as a lecturer, teaching spirituality at Redcliffe College here in England. We met because of our shared passion for spiritual formation, and I have benefited so much from our conversations about the nature of the Christian life and how to live it. Many of these deep exchanges happened over coffee at motorway service stations (we live at opposite ends of the country), and it was at one such meeting that the idea for this book was conceived.

God among the Ruins deals with the ever-present dilemma of why bad things happen to good people, but from a personal perspective rather than a detached, theoretical standpoint. At some point in life, many of us will know what it is to have the bottom fall out of our world, when circumstances shake our faith to the core. For Mags, the shaking began with the news that her beloved niece Jenny was diagnosed with a serious and rare form of cancer. Throughout the awfulness of Jenny's treatment, Mags was forced to wrestle with some of the most fundamental questions of faith: where is God in this? Why does he allow such things to happen? Why doesn't he answer our prayers? And then, when Jenny passed away, other questions rose to the surface. Would she ever be able to make sense of what had happened? Would her relationship with God ever be the same again?

This is an intensely personal book in which Mags shares with us her journey during that difficult time and beyond. She speaks openly and honestly about her fears, her doubts and her questions. She invites us into her world, into her mind and her heart, so that we can share the journey with her. We feel her pain, sense her bewilderment, but also follow her path to recovery – the rebuilding of her trust in God and the emergence of hope following her despair.

It was my privilege, along with some others, to be a small part of this journey and to watch from a distance the resilience of her faith as she processed what had happened with courage and integrity. After a couple of years had passed and I sensed she was ready, I asked Mags if she would write a short chapter about her experience for my book, *Deep Calls to Deep* (BRF, 2015), since the topic was about spiritual formation in the hard places of life. With a little coaxing she agreed, and I have to say I think her chapter is the best part of the book! I realised then that she has a gift for writing and that there was a much fuller story to be told. Here it is!

What I love about *God among the Ruins* is that it is so biblical in its approach. In the Bible, Mags found a surprising companion for her journey in the obscure Old Testament prophet called Habakkuk. His faith struggle gave Mags a framework for her own wrestling with God, and here she invites us to share her interaction with this ancient prophet. I read her text with my Bible in hand, and it made the book of Habakkuk come alive for me.

There is so much hope here, for this is a story of spiritual formation and the transformation that happens when we allow God to work in us during our times of pain, disorientation and loss. Ruins can be rebuilt with time, and recovery is possible. We are changed, and will never be the same again, but we can emerge from our times of darkness stronger than we were before. This is the testimony that Mags shares with us, not in a triumphalist way, but in humility and with candour. Her story will bring hope and healing to many.

Mags has written a very practical book, designed to help us reflect on our lives and enable us to process our pain. She has the mind of a teacher and the heart of a counsellor. After each chapter, there are helpful exercises to apply the teaching. Those who take the time to work through them will benefit enormously.

This is not a book to read as quickly as you can. Take your time and allow the book to read you. That way you will reap great rewards, both now and in the future, for yourself and for those for whom you care.

Tony Horsfall

Introduction

I'd slept deeply but woke suddenly, fully awake, aware of five words pulsing gently and insistently in my mind.

'Even though… even here… Emmanuel. Even though… even here… Emmanuel.'

As I burrowed more deeply into the warmth of the duvet, my mind began to drift over scriptures I knew which contained those words. David's words in Psalm 23 came to mind, '*Even though* I walk through the darkest valley… you are with me' (v. 4, NIV). Job's agonised declaration that, '*Though* he slay me, yet will I hope in him' (Job 13:15, NIV). The psalmist's discovery, recorded for us in Psalm 139, that whether the circumstances of his life took him to great depths or to great heights, whether his life was expansive or narrow, in darkness as in light – *even here* God was present, Emmanuel, God with us, was present (v. 10).

And then familiar words from the end of the book of Habakkuk: *Even though* the fig tree does not blossom, *even though* there is no fruit on the vine… yet I will rejoice (Habakkuk 3:17–18).

As I began to reflect on these 'even though's, I realised that each one was a declaration of trust and hope and confidence in distressing or devastating circumstances. This last scripture particularly stirred something deep within me. I remembered so little about the book of Habakkuk, but there was something about his defiant 'even though's in the face of such obvious loss that drew me out of bed that dawning morning. A full pot of coffee, my favourite throw, a comfy sofa, my Bible and a pen later, and I was ready to walk with Habakkuk.

I turned to those last verses again and I could almost hear Habakkuk's voice asserting,

> *Even though* the fig trees have no blossoms,
>   and there are no grapes on the vines;
> *even though* the olive crop fails,
>   and the fields lie empty and barren;
> *even though* the flocks die in the fields,
>   and the cattle barns are empty,
> *yet* I will rejoice in the Lord!
>   I will be joyful in the God of my salvation!
> The Sovereign Lord is my strength!
> HABAKKUK 3:17–19

They were defiantly hope-laden words in the face of devastating circumstances, of loss and need, of ruined work and failed expectations.

How had he come into such a hopeful place? I couldn't remember, so I turned to the beginning of this little book and after the very briefest of introductions was confronted with the words:

> How long, O Lord, must I call for help?
>   But you do not listen!
> 'Violence is everywhere!' I cry,
>   but you do not come to save…
> 〉 Why must I watch all this misery?
> HABAKKUK 1:2–3

I flipped to the end again and checked the verses – and back again to the beginning. Questions began to form even as the sun rose: how did he get from the outraged questions of the opening verses to the outpourings of confident hope in the closing words? What was the route he took? Where were the pathways he'd left? And where was God in it all?

These were not academic questions, but ones for which I was desperate for answers. I needed some kind of deepened hope, some kind of help that might ease the heavy ache of grief I had been carrying for over two years, a pain I had no inkling was coming when I arrived at my mum's home for the weekend in November 2010.

As I carried my bags in from the car, I was feeling happy to be home with mum, looking forward to a weekend of watching her favourite TV programmes with her, looking forward too to seeing my sister and her family for a good catch up on all their news.

My mother must have heard the car arrive because when I opened the front door she was waiting for me in the hallway; she looked grey and old – and scared. And my heart began to pound. She said nothing, but tried to pull me into the sitting room. 'What's wrong? What is it?' My mouth had gone dry as my mind flooded with the thought that her cancer, which had been in remission for six years, had returned. Her eyes searched my face, and in a cracked voice, 'Jenny, Jenny has cancer; it's very bad.'

Jenny, my wonderful 22-year-old niece, the daughter I never had and whom I loved with all of my heart, had *cancer*? There had to be a mistake. This could not be true; this could *not* be true.

'I need to go'. Leaving mum, I got back into the car and drove to my sister's home just a few minutes away. It was only when I saw her ravaged face that the awful truth of mum's words truly hit.

My sister is a nurse, working in cancer research. She knew the awful seriousness of Jenny's cancer. Quietly, through tears, she explained to me that Jenny didn't just have cancer, which would already have been hard to hear, she had an extremely rare, horrifyingly aggressive and deadly form of cancer. And there was no cure.

That was the beginning.

Over the next twelve months, Jenny would undergo multiple therapy treatments: radiotherapy, chemotherapy, brachytherapy, all endured by her in an effort to delay the spread of the cancer. But the disease was a monster which kept metastasising. Month by month, she got worse. Every therapy failed; nothing seemed to halt the onslaught, the strident encroachment of this disease. Jenny's body seemed to be a playground for this cancer as it spread into her organs, her spine, her lymph system. No part of her body was off limits to this insidious spread.

Through it all, Jenny was her wonderful self: optimistic, non-self-pitying, unselfish, funny, generous, beautiful. Through it all, I cried, prayed, claimed promises for healing, for comfort, for help, for salvation. I declared the truth of God's character; owned for myself the words of the psalmist in Psalm 86:5, 'You are so good… so full of unfailing love for all who ask for your help.' And verse 15, 'You… are a God of compassion and mercy… filled with unfailing love and faithfulness.' This was my God, this was my Saviour, and knowing his power on behalf of the weak and the helpless, I did what that psalmist had done as recorded in Psalm 88:13, 'I keep on pleading day by day', trusting that God would one day reveal with a flourish his healing hand – and Jenny would be freed from this cancer.

But nothing happened.

Through it all, faithful friends walked with me, prayed with me and for me, trusted for me, wrote cards and emails, and held me up on the many days when I could not hold myself up, when curling up into a tight ball seemed to be the best option for coping with the day.

Over the months, as Jenny became worse, I sought out those who seemed to have the gift of faith and asked them to pray, but it seemed that every time people prayed, she got worse, so after a while I stopped sharing prayer requests, and I stopped asking people to pray. But I carried on quietly, secretly, hoping, trusting, for a miracle.

It took just over a year for the cancer to win the battle. In the last week of her life, Jenny's pain intensified beyond morphine's ability to keep up, and now my prayer became a pleading that God would take her. She had endured so much and not been healed, but could he now at least ease her passing. She was in pain, in distress, confused and so, so weary of it all. And still she lived on, and on.

On the night she died, I kissed her goodnight, whispered that I would see her in the morning and drove home to mum. It was late and she had already gone to bed, so I crept up to my room and there through clenched teeth I howled my rage at God. I pleaded for her release, I irrationally cajoled with promises of fulfilling whatever sacrifice was necessary for me. I groaned my agony, and unbelievably, I threatened God; I threatened him that even though I would not, could not, stop believing in him, I would stop loving him; I would stop trusting his heart if he did not now have mercy on her. The pain-pounded irrationality poured out of me.

At five minutes past midnight, as I lay exhausted on my bed, my nephew phoned to say that she had gone. Jenny had died. The impossible, the stupid, the cruel, the senseless had happened. And while my mother slept, unknowing, I buried my face in my pillow and sobbed my pain and my grief. Drained of everything, I waited in the darkness for the dawn, hugging tight, rocking the news that no grandmother should have to hear.

Over the next days, both my thankfulness at Jenny's release and my outrage at the wickedness of her death poured out of me. Although there were moments of profound thankfulness, outrage seemed to be the primary emotion of those days, the walls of my tiny bedroom amazingly withstanding the onslaught of my whispered fury as I retreated there when I could no longer handle being around the many people who called with flowers and condolences and baskets of memories to share with us.

And then, the evening before her funeral, I sat in the car in the driveway of mum's home and with my head on the steering wheel, I surrendered. The fight was all gone, the rage spent. I was depleted of all energy. And I let go. I let go of blaming God for how Jenny died; I let go of blaming him for not answering so many, many prayers; I let go of his needing to 'work this together for good' for me or for my family in order for Jenny's death to have any dignity or purpose. Basically, I let go of God needing to be anything other than who I'd come to know him to be over so many years; my dearest friend, my loving, faithful Father. Quietly and very calmly, I spoke to my God, 'I have nowhere else to go. There is no way out of this, there is only a way through it, and I choose to go through it with you. But you have to be more.' I hardly knew what I meant by that last phrase. But his love interpreted what I could barely articulate and in the depths of my heart I sensed a clear response, 'More I can do', and then very clearly, I sensed these gentle words: 'Mags, you have always trusted me as the God you know, now I am asking you to trust me as the God you no longer recognise.'

Memories flooded in. Through the years I had come to know the Lord as good and kind and loving; he was my compassionate, tender God; the God of mercy and generous grace. Through hard times of deep disappointment, devastating loss, betrayal and dream-crushing circumstances, I had known and experienced his loving kindness and the depth of his comfort. I really had. But after these battle-torn months of bruisingly unanswered prayer, I had been faced with a God I hardly recognised. The clouds of grief and fear and pain had distorted his features; I could barely make out his outline through the veil of tears I lived with every day. The God I thought I knew, the one I loved, had become a mystery to me. I no longer recognised him, and now, in the quietness of my car, on that last day of November 2011, a whispered question rose in my heart, 'Who *are* you?' and the answer was immediate and clear. In the very depths of my soul, I heard him whisper, 'I am your Emmanuel; I am God *with* you; I *am* God with you.'

And then peace, at least in that quiet moment, that quietest of evenings before the morning of Jenny's funeral. No healing, no resurrection, no miracle – except perhaps this miracle of peace.

He had broken through with the promise of his presence, and it was enough.

It had been a long year since Jenny's death, a year since her funeral when almost 1,000 people turned up, each wearing or carrying a flash of yellow, Jenny's favourite colour, and each one expressing the grief of their own hearts over the loss of such an amazingly joyful presence in the world. And as a family we grieved, each in our own way.

And I grieved; every single day of that year had brought new depths of missing her, new depths of pain for the loss of her. Her absence was present everywhere. There were moments when I thought that if I could just figure out a reason for it all, if I could just turn 'Why?' into a more pragmatic 'What now?', then I would find more peace. But in the midst of this splintering grieving, wise friends advised me not to try and make sense of Jenny's death, not to search for a lesson to learn or a purpose to settle into which would perhaps ease the weight of grief for the moment; not yet. That time would come but, for now, the wisest action was to wait quietly with God, for God, trusting that at some stage in the months or perhaps even years ahead, hope would appear again, healing would soothe its way to my heart and the questions answered – or not, at least in this world. The desperate need to determine a purpose for her death needed to be released right now, surrendered into the care of God who would hold the questions until I was ready for the answers – if there were any. I could not even begin to imagine what shape hope might take, what dimensions healing might hold, what possible purpose Jenny's death might serve that her life wouldn't serve equally well. But I did wait, holding and being held by the words I had sensed him speak in the car that evening – words which invited me to trust in the dark what I had always believed about him in the light; to trust and to lean into one word, *Emmanuel*, and all the richness that word contained.

Just a few months before the Lord's early morning wakeup call, I had come across words written by Eric Liddell, the Olympic runner who became a missionary and who died in a Japanese prisoner of war camp in World War II. They resonated deeply within me, sparking the hope of healing and new life:

> Circumstances may appear to wreck our lives and God's plans, but God is not helpless among the ruins.[1]

And slowly, over the months, I had been experiencing this gentle moving of God among the ruins. He *was* beginning to heal my broken heart, waking me to a cold December dawn with these words from Habakkuk's own grieving and healing heart; words of defiant hope; words which would become a gift for me to unwrap in the months that followed. Somehow, unbelievably, Habakkuk had found his way back to life, to joy, to hope and to a vibrant confidence in God. How did he do it? Where did this determination to live with such explosive energy come from? I was intrigued and, more, hopeful.

On that morning, as I sat there hugging my coffee mug and looking over the rooftops at the sky getting lighter, I drew my journal closer and wrote, 'I so admire Habakkuk's honesty, his humility, his wisdom and his hopefulness. I have a deep sense that he'll be a wise companion for my own journey in the months ahead.'

And he has been. The circumstances of our stories were different, but the confusion and bewilderment and disappointment and the ragged grief of it all were the same. In his story I found snatched echoes of my own, which helped me make sense of where I'd been and where this journey might take me. The account of his honest struggles helped me to understand something of my own. His words of lament validated my own cries. His questions reflected my own questions. His courage and honesty invited me to dig even deeper, to discover the wells of my own courage and honesty. His hopefulness challenged me so many times to trust the slow unwrapping of the purposes of God in my life. As I studied his words and his actions,

I recognised places and practices that had been life-giving and God-affirming for me too and was encouraged to continue to strengthen them. It's been a few years now since that early morning discovery, but even today I am finding that the companionship of this obscure prophet on my continued journey toward healing and trust and transformation is as inspiring and as wise as ever.

The pages that follow therefore are in some ways a tapestry of moments and movements, interwoven threads of two journeys; the thread of Habakkuk's story as he walked with God through the awfulness of his reality, and the thread of my own reflections through the journey of Jenny's cancer and her death. My prayer is that the thread of *your own* journey will find a place in this tapestry as you weave your own reflections, your own practices, within the fabric of these words.

At the end of each chapter are some suggestions for reflection – a pause for thought, like the one below, or a spiritual practice or prayer form to engage with which hopefully will help us move more surely toward the God whom Habakkuk knew, and the God who knows us so very well, and who truly is with us among the ruins of our lives.

Reflection:
Even though… even here… Emmanuel

Habakkuk's 'even though's are a snapshot of a world in which the blessing of God seems to have been removed. What is left is massive loss: the failure of crops, the death of animals, the devastation of the land were all evidences of the removal of God's blessing on his people. And yet… In the face of all of this loss, Habakkuk holds on to the truth that the covenant God of Israel cannot and will not abandon his people. He continues to be present even through the losses, even through the destruction and the distress. Because of his trust in the truth of God's covenant word, Habakkuk makes this defiant declaration of trust: 'Yet I will rejoice…'

Before we begin our journey with Habakkuk, it might be helpful for us to identify any 'even though… even here' places in our own lives, and to invite the Lord to lead us into a fuller understanding and experience of his name, Emmanuel.

So, you may want to write or make an audio recording of your reflections on the following questions:

- Where are the 'even though' places in your own life right now, those places where your faith is being challenged, your hope stretched, your understanding of God and how God works confused or bewildering? Where is that 'even though' place in your life that you sense God may be inviting you to trust him? What would trusting him in that place look like? What would need to change in your thinking or praying or being or doing in order to walk in trust in this place?

- Is there an 'even here' place in your life, a place in which you can hardly imagine that God would be, could be, present? Are there circumstances, relationships, inner struggles and outer demands which seem to you at times to be even beyond God's reach to help you in them? A place too deep or too far for him to go to? The psalmist in Psalm 139 had obviously thought about this and his conclusion in verse 10 was that 'even there your hand will guide me, and your strength will support me'. What would God's guiding, God's support look like for you in your 'even here' place?

- What does God's name 'Emmanuel' communicate to you? As you look back on your journey with God, when have you experienced the reality of 'Emmanuel' in the different places of your life? What difference do you sense the presence of Emmanuel would make to the 'even though… even here' places of your life?

Before moving on into the rest of the book, you might want to pause for a few moments to consciously place yourself in the presence of the God who knows your life, your heart, your journey, and who promises to be *your* Emmanuel for all that is needed.

You might find it helpful to bring to the Lord all your reflections in a prayer which begins with the words, *My Emmanuel…*

Chapter 1

It's a long and winding road

Faith is better understood as a verb than as a noun, as a process than as a possession. Faith is not being sure where you're going but going anyway. A journey without maps.
Frederick Buechner[2]

I will lead the blind by ways they have not known,
   along unfamiliar paths I will guide them.
ISAIAH 42:16 (NIV)

It was the end of the class and my students were chatting happily as they left the room. It had been weeks since Jenny's diagnosis, weeks of chemotherapy and radiotherapy, weeks of brutal treatment, weeks of seemingly unanswered prayer. I had told my students nothing of this, nothing of Jenny, nothing of what our family was going through. I was carrying on as normal, and appeared as normal as ever – or so I thought.

Very quietly, Tim approached the lectern, holding out a scrappy piece of paper, torn from a corner of his lecture notes.

'Um, I just wanted to give you this.' And he shuffled out of the room.

I opened up the creased scrap, and on it were scribbled words which immediately brought tears to my eyes: 'For this I have Jesus.' Such simple words, but a gift from the God who *saw* me that morning, and who spoke through the kindness of this tender-hearted student who knew nothing of where I was coming from, nothing of what was going on in my life, but who did know how to respond to the gentle nudging of a compassionate God.

For *this* I have Jesus; for *this* very circumstance, *this* very pain, Jesus. The truth of this statement became a tensile thread in the fabric of the next months as I witnessed the battle for Jenny's life. Jesus would be with me, *in* it all, *through* it all, in ways I could scarcely have imagined in that moment of emptied-room silence. Through the words on that scrap of paper, there was a hint of the truth that the God who wept at the tomb of his friend Lazarus saw and understood my own tears. The God who provided manna from heaven for his children in the desert would provide words from his own heart to sustain my soul in the months to come as I made my own way through the desert of loss which lay ahead. There would be words, beacon-lights, for the dark and unfamiliar paths I was yet to walk down.

In the introduction to his translation of the book of Habakkuk in THE MESSAGE Bible, Eugene Peterson writes,

> Most prophets, most of the time, speak God's word to us… But Habakkuk speaks our words to God. He gives voice to our bewilderment, articulates our puzzled attempts to make sense of things, faces God with our disappointment with God… Habakkuk started out exactly where we start out with our puzzled complaints and God-accusations, but he didn't stay there.[3]

It's the words 'but he didn't stay there' which reflect the wonder and the hope of Habakkuk's journey. Martin Lloyd Jones titled his commentary on Habakkuk *From Fear to Faith*; Warren Wiersbe entitles his book on Habakkuk, *From Worry to Worship*, both titles holding an implicit acknowledgment that the value of this wee book may lie in mapping the contours of Habakkuk's journey laid out in these three brief chapters. It was a journey which took him from perplexity to praise; from anguish to awe; from despair to dancing across the top of the mountains; from a narrow view of God and his involvement with the nation of Israel to an awareness that God was the God of all creation, the God who held the destiny of nations, not just the nation of Israel, in his hands. It's a breathtaking journey that draws us into the very heart of trust and of transformation.

This record of Habakkuk's journey opens a window for us into one man's struggle to make sense of his world and God's involvement in it when that world was falling apart. We become observers of the birth of hope through the labour pains of brokenness and distress. And I wonder if one of the reasons that this book has been preserved for us by the Holy Spirit is to give *us* hope and direction for those times when our own lives, or the lives of those we care about, are falling apart. When the control we thought we had over our lives is revealed to be an illusion, and there is an unravelling of our carefully stewarded dreams, Habakkuk's journey may give us hope and confidence for our own journey. Although it may have begun in anger and in anguish, in doubt and with a fistful of questions, it ended with confident rejoicing. Eventually. The transformation which took place in Habakkuk's life was the outcome of a *process*; he was not simply transported from grief to glory in the wave of a holy wand. There was no short cut. There was no passing 'Go' on the Monopoly board of his life. There was no little ladder easing him up on to a higher plane of maturity. There was just this ongoing journey of trust in God and transformation by God from a starting point he would never have willingly chosen.

Richard Rohr writes,

> Normally there has to be a precipitating event that leads to transformation. I call it the 'stumbling stone', using a biblical term. Your two-plus-two world has to fail you, has to fall apart. Business as usual doesn't work. Usually that involves something very personal: suffering or failure or humiliation.[4]

For Habakkuk, the precipitating event that would lead eventually to his own transformation seems to begin with the apparent silence of God in the face of his agonised pleas for a response to his prayers. Confronted with the ever-increasing wickedness of his people,

Habakkuk wanted God to intervene in redemptive ways. He wanted a God who was involved. He got what he wanted, but perhaps not in the way he wanted it. And so the journey began.

The writer of the book of Hebrews exhorts each one of us to run the particular race that is set before us (Hebrews 12:1). In this particular race, we are not called to race against anyone, or to run anyone else's race; we are to engage with our own race. We are invited to live out our own unique journey of faith with God; a journey which will take time and effort on our part. Our quick-fix instant-access culture works hard to communicate the message that there is always an easier, quicker way to do things – even the transformation of our lives into men and women who reflect the character of Christ in all its rich depth and beauty. There may be an impression that if we can just attend enough motivating gatherings and listen to enough inspiring speakers, if we read the latest Christian blockbuster, and receive daily devotionals from our favourite Christian author, then somehow, by a process of spiritual osmosis which doesn't require any real effort of engagement on our part, we will enter into a profound depth of faith and be dramatically and painlessly transformed, avoiding the messiness and the necessity of the *process* of transformation. But we can't. The journey beckons for us as it did for Habakkuk, and as it's done for countless others before us.

Contoured beauty

Perhaps one of our difficulties in accepting the realities of the journey is that we don't expect it! We are rarely taught that life with God involves moving through a variety of landscapes and through the characteristics of all four seasons. Years ago, when I began my walk with God, I naively assumed that the path on which I walked would take me on a linear ascent to glory; a happy trek of trusting faith along a straight and smooth and upwardly inclining road. My biggest responsibility, therefore, was to ensure that I didn't fall off the path through sin or disobedience or a lack of faith. God had shown me the path of life and my job was to stay on it with all the effort I could muster. And as long as I did my part, God would do his and the road would lead straight to glory. It was an incredibly nerve-wracking way to live, because rather than becoming broader and more generous in its dimensions, the path seemed to become more and more narrow the longer I was on it until it became high-wire thin, and walking in obedient faith became a life-threatening experience!

It was never communicated to me, at least not in a way that I understood, that this path could be contoured in any way; that it would lead through valleys as well as mountain tops; that it would pass through desert stretches and lose itself in rushing rivers. Neither did I know that just as there are physical seasons there are also spiritual seasons which correspond to the seasons we experience in the northern hemisphere at least. I never knew that winter times of quiet and seeming barrenness are as normal and as necessary to the spiritual life as the joyful spring-like budding of new hope and learning and life. The impression I had picked up was that, in the Christian life lived under the blessing of God, it was always summer!

It never occurred to me that there was anything wrong with this picture that I'd picked up – except for the dissonant reality that, try as I might, I couldn't make this kind of life work. I seemed to go three steps forward and two steps back. Some days I fought sin and some days I just gave in. Some days my walk with God really did seem to be bathed in sunshine and other days the clouds of boredom or disappointment or weariness were my reality. So I hid behind layers of activity and an enthusiastic façade, and trusted that no one would penetrate my disguise and discover the real me hiding behind the day's mask of choice. In those early days of my Christian life, I desperately wanted to belong to the Christian group where I was learning so much about discipleship and growth. I wanted so much to fit in with the men and women I was around, who seemed to live such whole and holy lives in the sunshine of their sure and certain faith. What I didn't know then was that they looked at me in the same way that I looked at them, and none of us ever told the truth that there were times when we wondered if it was true; if there really was a God, and if there was, did it matter anyway?

The reality laid out for us in the scriptures clearly demonstrates that we do not walk a perfectly paved road from our earliest awakenings to the grace of God, straight through the gates of glory and into the New Jerusalem. This just doesn't happen. It is an illusion to believe that it does, but it is an illusion perpetuated by teachings which seem to convey that there is no room for failure or doubt or questioning or anger or fear in a God-pursuing, God-blessed life. It's further perpetuated by well-meaning testimonies which only share the good bits of a life with God in the mistaken belief that to share the real story, the harder, struggling, backstory to the testimony would somehow diminish God's glory. And then there's worship which focuses exclusively on praise and thanksgiving, and sadly glosses over the need that most of us have, to be led to the throne of grace and given permission to stand there as the broken, confused and sometimes doubting men and women that we are.

Tragically, this airbrushed portrayal of a life lived with God, a life of following Jesus, does not reflect the reality of the life of Jesus himself, who made his final journey to the cross stumbling and forsaken, crushed under the weight of wood and sorrow, unrelieved and unrescued, and who died with a question on his lips.

In reading the experiences of the men and women of faith and in reflecting on my own journey, it is clear that the reality of our lives bears witness to the truth that the path of our faith-lives is as contoured as the landscape around us. And this is normal; it is human; it is biblical.

I am privileged to live on the edge of the Cotswolds. It's an area of outstanding beauty, not just because of the presence of scattered villages of mellow honey-stoned cottages nestling in quiet valleys, or the wild flower meadows and luminous fields of yellow rape, but because of the very contours of the land itself. Standing recently high on a hill near to where I live, my breath was taken away by the view stretching out before me: right in front of me and way into the distance were gently undulating hills and valleys, sweeping vistas of green chequered plains, a sparkling ribbon of river threading its way through sheep-grazed meadows, and craggy-rocked ridges speared with trees which stretched up, unbelievably tall, into clouds. It was awesomely beautiful. Over millennia, this landscape had been hewn out of ice and floods and the movements of rock and ridge. The earth had been nourished by life-giving rain and by the dying of leaves and small animals. Sunshine and showers had played their part in shaping the awesome beauty that lay before me. Worship could be the only response to such beauty – and high on that hill I stretched out my arms and worshipped the God whose handiwork, whose craftwork, was revealed in such beauty, such an awesome landscape.

And yet the shaping of the spiritual landscape of our own lives can be so confusing as we misjudge our valley times as unequivocal evidence of our failure and/or God's disfavour, and our mountaintop moments as equally unequivocal evidence of his blessing on our faithfulness. There *are* mountaintop experiences of joy-infused blessing, but there are times too when we journey through a landscape of deep valleys and shadowed paths where little light seems to penetrate. There *are* times when we can clearly see and sense the rivers of the Spirit of God flowing freely through our lives, but then there are times when that water seems to pool and stagnate, or dry up completely. There are days of delight and days of drudgery; days when we feel dead and days when we feel totally alive – and the experiences of *all* of these days are part of the shaping of the landscape of our journeys with God. One day is no more sinful or God-abandoned than another for it being harder to handle, because it brings tears instead of smiles. To expect otherwise is to live a Pollyanna life.

Jesus was so very real, so honest with his disciples about the reality of living in this world. In his last moments with them, he reassured them that even though they would experience trouble and suffering, pressure and stress in the world, they did not need to be afraid because he would be with them (John 16:33). Jesus' disciples already knew the truth of the reality of the constant pressure of the world, but they also needed to know the corresponding truth of the reality of the constant presence of Christ with them in that very world. Before he finally left them, Jesus promised his disciples that he would always be with them; they would never be without his presence (Matthew 28:20). We are the heirs to that promise of his presence and we need to hold tight this same assurance, the same understanding, that there may be days which are pressured and stressed, laced with suffering and crushing trouble, days when we stand with uplifted faces to the skies, in the rubbled ruins of our dreams, our reputations, our dearest relationships. And that at those very moments, covered in the dust of our distress, even here, in this place, Jesus our Emmanuel, God, is *with us* and comes alongside us to walk with us, in and through that very landscape. We are not abandoned. We are not lost without a guide. We are held in his sight and in his love. We are gripped by his hand. He knows the way; he is the way. And he *will* lead us through.

Moving times

In his studies of Psalms,[5] theologian and scholar Walter Brueggemann charts a journey through the psalms which is reflective of our own journey through life with God. In his studies, he observed that there seemed to be two recurring movements through which the psalmists travelled; the movement from settledness to unsettledness, and the movement from unsettledness to a new settledness. The places from which these movements originate he labelled as 'Orientation', 'Disorientation' and 'New Orientation'. Orientation is that happy place where we sense that God is in his heaven and everything is right in the world. Disorientation is the disturbingly unsettled place where there seems to be a real shaking of everything that felt safe and secure about our faith, our understanding of God and how life with God works. A sense of disillusionment, darkness and lostness is common in this place. Finally, there is New Orientation, a place where, for no apparent reason, we experience a surprising lightness, a breakthrough of new hope, and a joy-sprinkled anticipation of good things to come.

To understand that these three places, these two movements, are a natural part of the ebb and flow of our journey with God can be such a relief. Right now, each one of us is living in one of these three places, and there will come a time when each of us will experience these movements. Like the natural flowing of the tides, these movements will recur throughout our journey with God. When we first encounter Habakkuk in the opening words of the book, he is clearly in that place of Disorientation where his understanding of God and his purposes is unravelling, where he is confused and bewildered and where he has more questions than answers. Through the rest of the book, we witness his journey into a place of New Orientation which springboards him into the future with new hope and energy.

Looking back

In Romans 15:4 (NIV), Paul writes, 'For everything that was written in the past was written to teach us, so that through the endurance taught in the Scriptures and the encouragement they provide, we might have hope.' The pages of our Bibles are littered with the accounts of men and women who have journeyed with God. Their examples are meant to provide us with encouragement and hope as we embark on our own journeys. The accounts of the heroes of Hebrews 11, for example, provide us with models who are wise and worthy travelling companions for our own journeys. As we track their journeys, we glean so much for our own journeys of faith.

We watch Abraham responding to God's invitation to leave his home in the metropolitan city of Ur, to leave the gods who were so familiar to him there and to step out with a newly revealed God who was calling him into an unknown future. Abraham's journey took him from security and safety and the known into the cavernous expanse of the unknown, where nothing was guaranteed except the promise of a God who appeared to him and pushed wide open the edges of his world.

Hundreds of years later, the Moabite widow Ruth made a very similar journey as she left her parents' home, her village, her friends and the life she knew, to walk with an embittered and lonely old woman into a future in which she would take her place in the lineage of the Messiah himself. It was a journey of love and amazing courage.

We may be so familiar with the story of the exodus and the desert wanderings of the children of God that we miss the truth that this journey was not just a physical journey over 40 years of desert living; it was a journey of attitude-shaping transformation; from slavery and external obedience to authority and into freedom and an inner response of love to a covenant God. It was a journey from rules to relationship. Rules are pretty safe – 'Do this and you shall live' – but God was moving them into the risky realm of *relationship* with him, where they would learn that life in all its fullness would be theirs as they embraced and entrusted themselves to the strength of the love of God for them. It was completely new territory in more ways than one.

And then there's Job. Over the years, I'd read the book of Job many times, but it wasn't until Jenny's death that I began to appreciate the stunning depths of his loss, and the depths, too, of his courage to continue to hold on to God; to trust, and to believe that there was hope for his life beyond the agony of this present pain and confusion and grief; to believe that God was present and moving among the very real ruins of his life. He was financially ruined as his herds and flocks were decimated, his reputation ruined in a culture which equated wealth and prosperity with the visible rewards of God for righteousness. His body too was wretched as he sat and scraped his boils in the ash heap which so represented his life at that moment. And worst of all, his whole family, except for a deeply wounded and aggrieved wife, had been wiped out in a single devastating disaster.

His whole life wrecked, he nevertheless searched for God among the literal and emotional ruins of his life, refusing to let go of the shrouded *mystery* of God and his purposes. His trusting tenacity was a profound act of heroism in the face of the dogmatic, confidence-edged words of his counsellors. His humble wisdom is particularly evident in the words, 'Lo, these are but the outskirts of his ways: And how small a whisper do we hear of him!' Job 26:14 (ASV).

Job's wisdom had been hewn from the rock of his own suffering. Through the blinding confusion of his grief, he recognised that at most he saw the edges, the horizon line of God's ways; he heard only the faintest whisper of God. Through the shattering experience of his losses and the very real silence of God in response to the cry and questions of those losses, Job was aware that what he saw and heard of God's actions and purposes, what he knew of God, were just the outer fringes of who God really was. Through his experience, Job had become deeply aware that God was greater and more mysterious and unknowable than he had ever recognised.

In our own journeys with God, if we walk long enough, we discover this same truth for ourselves: we reach one horizon and get ready to celebrate, only to discover that what we thought was the end is actually just a ridge, and there is far more to know; a vast expanse of God and his ways that has yet to be discovered. We come to discover that any journey toward God or with God will always be a journey further and further beyond the edges and the outskirts of what we already know, because God is constantly drawing us on, drawing us in, further and more deeply, into the vast reaches of the dimensions of who he is, and into his purposes. Through the very circumstances of our lives, God is constantly and consistently inviting us into a trust-packed journey with him, where the borders of what we know and what we have experienced of him are being continually stretched and enlarged, allowing the life of Christ within us space to breathe in ever more profoundly transformative ways. It is so richly different from the single-laned, high-hedged A-road to glory we may have been taught!

Centuries ago, around the edges of maps, the words 'There be dragons!' would be written by mapmakers. Those words signified the end of what had already been discovered and mapped and pinned down. Beyond the known was a dangerous place – and it was best not to go there. And in our own lives, we may have that same response; we may sense within us an invitation from God, a drawing into a new place, beyond the horizons of what we've always known, always believed, always trusted to be true; and we may draw back, fearful that to go beyond those horizons may place us in danger.

So we resist, not only out of fear, but also because we sense that it might be too uncomfortable and perhaps too costly to respond to such an invitation. Some of us may even doubt that there can be anything beyond what we already know, and we may stand with Galileo's inquisitors, insisting that to believe there is another way to look at our world, our faith, our God, that there is anything beyond what we have already been taught and believe, might actually be heresy. Our very certainties can harden us to the possibility that there may be new things to discover about God and about life with him that we have yet to experience. So we resist; beyond the horizon there may be the 'dragons' of different understandings of God which we have never before seriously encountered; there may be new perspectives on familiar scriptures; issues that have seemed so black and white might actually be grey(ish). And we can get scared; scared that we might fall off the edge of our known and safe world into a place inhabited by dragons, or worse, perhaps, by others who have fallen. And there will be no way back.

Some years ago my friend Tracy confronted me with the trajectory in which my dearly held, narrow-boundaried convictions might be taking me. I've never forgotten her words, spoken thoughtfully over a quiet lunch in a Cheshire pub. She said, 'Mags, be very careful that your convictions don't harden into a dogmatism that doesn't allow for doubt.' Tracy's comment nailed a subconscious fear I had of being anything less than 100 per cent certain of everything. I wrongly equated certainty with faith and I so wanted to be faithfull. But interestingly, I don't see 100 per cent certainty in the lives of our heroes of faith; what I do see is a willingness to trust and to move forward with God into the unknown.

If we chart the faith journeys of these heroes, as unique as they are, we notice that there are certain common features which tend to emerge which we can use as landmarks for our own journeys of trust and transformation.

Features of the journey

Perhaps the first thing to notice is that the movement of their journeys was initiated by God, either directly through revelation and his spoken word, or indirectly through people or circumstances. I think of Israel in the wilderness and God's training of them to follow the cloud, to follow the pillar when it moved. These were God-directed moves. Through the leadership of Moses, God had led them into the wilderness and into all that place held of grief and glory; behind it all was the initiative of God, but Moses was the embodiment of that initiative.

Each journey also seemed to invite and demand a willingness to let go; and in particular to let go of control. In so many of these journeys there seems to be a movement from control to lack of control, and a willingness to accept God's control of the situation. Allied with this, each person or group's journey involved the willingness to be dependent, not independent: to be dependent on God's word and the promise of his presence, to be dependent too on others and on their strengths, their giftedness, when the need called for it.

There was mystery and trust involved in the journey too, because no matter how favoured and faithful they may have been, no matter their previous experience of God, the journey was never straightforward, and how God dealt with each one was a unique mystery. And the journeys resulted in transformation; these men and women were never the same after their journey with God. After the long process of trusting him with who they were, with their hearts and dreams and desires, they were just never the same.

As we walk with Habakkuk on his journey, we will encounter many of these features in the landscape through which he passes. And perhaps as we do, we will recognise them as features in the landscape of our own lives. And then we will be faced with a choice: to go forward into the unknown or to stay where we are, settled and secure, but missing the adventure of all that could yet be, beyond the horizon.

Reflection: On the journey

Habakkuk wasn't delivered from fear into faith, from rage into rejoicing in an instant of believing prayer, as wonderful as that is when it happens. He had to make the journey with God across the rocky-valleyed landscape of his fears and doubts and disappointments and grief. As we've already seen, Walter Brueggemann suggests that over a lifetime of walking with God, we will experience two distinct and separate movements into three places: Orientation, Disorientation and New Orientation.

It may be helpful for us to unwrap the characteristics of each place in a little more detail: a key characteristic in the place of Orientation is the word 'congruence'. We experience a congruence between what we read about God in his word and what we experience in our lives. We read that God is a faithful provider and that's just what we experience in our lives. Emerging out of this congruence is a sense of well-being and contentment, peace, a hopefulness about life. We experience God as good, faithful, loving, kind, present. Although there may be challenges and difficulties, we are confident of God's help and presence with us in them.

In Disorientation, a key characteristic is incongruity; God may be described as a light in darkness, as a protector, as a loving presence in our lives, but our actual experience of God is the opposite – God is absent, non-answering and hidden. There is confusion, bewilderment and distress. We are in the pit and it is deep and dark. And incredibly lonely.

In the place of New Orientation, key characteristics are a sense of surprise, newness, freshness, new hopefulness, relief, release. There is a bold expectation of the future.

- Think back to three years ago; which of the above places was 'home' for you at that time? How would you characterise that place in your life? What words would best describe it? What was going on in your life at the time which contributed to your being in this place? What was going on in your relationship with God at that time? What words best describe your experience of God at that time?

- Now, think about where you are today; where is 'home' for you? Has it changed from three years ago? If so, what words best characterise where you are now? What about your experience of God? What words best describe that right now?

- As you reflect on these two places, what events, new understandings, circumstances or relationships do you sense have contributed to moving between the two places you've identified above?

- In light of your reflections and what you've read in this chapter, what advice would you want to give to your journeying self as you continue into the future?

You might want to bring all of these thoughts together in a prayer, beginning perhaps with the words, 'God of my journey…' and see where those words lead you.

Chapter 2

Wounded ragings

O Lord, how long shall I cry for help,
 and you will not listen?
HABAKKUK 1:2–3, NRSV

Christians… may need explicit permission and
encouragement to grieve, shout and shake their fist at God,
as our Jewish forebears never hesitated to do. We have been
taught to be polite, even toward God, whereas what we
need is to be real, especially with God.
Marjorie J. Thompson[6]

After the briefest biographical note, brief perhaps because so little
seems to be known about this obscure prophet Habakkuk, we are
immediately confronted with words of total bewilderment, deep
disappointment, and outraged anger. 'O Lord, how long shall I cry
for help, and you will not listen?' he screams, and we are pulled,
headfirst, into the anguish of this man of God. He is confused,
anguished, bewildered, distressed and frustrated with God. And it
pours out of him in pounding questions and searing accusations.

The first words we hear from him are shocking words of unrestrained
assault upon God's character; he faces off with God and holds
nothing back. With complete abandonment he screams his grievance
at God, unwrapping in God's presence the tangle of circumstances
which has brought him to this point in his life, his faith.

Some historical background may help us here. It seems that
Habakkuk had lived through the rich legacy of the reign of good
King Josiah of Judah. After years of idolatry and corruption under a

succession of wicked kings, Judah experienced a revival of worship and holiness and justice under the godly Josiah. Habakkuk, who may have served in the temple in Jerusalem during this time, would have experienced days of blessing and growth as he took part in Judah's revival. But then the darkness descended again. Josiah was killed in battle and, in an unimaginable turn of events, the weak-natured, fickle Jehoiakim became king. In barely a few months, not only was there a return to the old idol-worshipping, God-abandoning pre-Josiah days, but even worse days as Jehoiakim brought into Judah the gods of the conquering nation, and seemingly greater corruption and dissolution and moral laxity that matched the excesses of the worst of Judah's kings in the past.

Habakkuk, reeling from these events, seems to be totally bewildered at the apparent inattention, inaction and lack of concern that God seems to be expressing. How could God have allowed such a reversal to occur? That such a good and godly man as Josiah was killed, Jehoiakim brought to the throne and all the good that Josiah had achieved – gone in a matter of months! How could this possibly have happened? Where was God in all of this? How long would God stay uninvolved? Was God really so unaware? Why wasn't he doing something? Couldn't he have stepped in and protected Josiah? There is so much at stake, and where is God?

Habakkuk is caught in a double whammy. In Hebrew, the book we know as Habakkuk is entitled 'The burden of Habakkuk,' and his burden was twofold: one is the burden of the situation in Judah; it is a situation over which he had absolutely no control; there was nothing he could do to make it any better – it was what it was and he was helplessly unable to effect any change. The second is the painful burden of God's seeming indifference to it all. We have no idea how long he had been praying about the situation before he started crying out to God so desperately. The Hebrew word translated very tamely as 'call' in our English Bibles is far more dramatic; it is a screaming, crying out, insistent call, a desperate shout. There is a sense in which he has reached breaking point. We are witnessing a man at the end of his tether; a man who has been praying to a silent God, whom he demands be silent no more.

In some ways, Habakkuk's situation reminds me of the account of the disciples in Mark's Gospel, who in the midst of a terrifying storm wake Jesus with the question, 'Teacher, don't you care that we are going to drown?' (Mark 4:38). Jesus was in the boat with them; he was present with them, but he is sleeping while they are sinking! You can almost hear their bewilderment: 'What is wrong with you? Don't you care?' Their words echo those of the psalmist in Psalm 44:23, who in frustration cries, 'Wake up O Lord! Why do you sleep?' And in essence, this is what Habakkuk is screaming at God: Don't you *care* about what is happening in the lives of your people? They are drowning in violence and wickedness, and where are you? Does it not bother you that the whole nation is being led like sheep to the slaughter? Do you not see the gross injustices all around you? Can you not see, can you not hear what is happening right under your nose in the temple, the appointed place of your people's encounter with you? Are you asleep?

I'm no artist, but if I were to paint a picture of the landscape that Habakkuk is inhabiting right now, I think I would paint it as a dark, tortured wilderness of a place, strewn with massive boulders and thorn-laid earth, with darkening storm-laden skies above. And the wonder of this man is that he is pushing his way *through* this landscape to reach the God he *knows* can act on behalf of his people.

Wrestling with God

This pushing through seems to be in Habakkuk's very nature. His name means 'embracer', or 'one who embraces,' but this is not an affectionate hug; it's more like the 'embrace' of wrestlers as they grapple with each other, hanging on for dear life. And this image seems to best describe Habakkuk; he is wrestling with God, a Jacob's desperate 'I will not let you go' kind of wrestling. He is not letting go; he is pulling God to him, jerking God towards his questions with tough, rough ropes of lament.

I had always understood lament to be primarily about sadness and tears, a kind of spiritual blues song, accompanied by tears and sung quietly in a minor key. But the books of Psalms and Lamentations clearly portray lament as more than broken-hearted weeping; it is also outrage and anger; it is grief and sorrow expressed not just in tears, but in complaints and gut-wrenching honesty with God about the realities of life. It is a depth of groaning.

True lament breaks open the depths of our hearts to God; it is an act of courageous faith which invites God to enter into the pain of that broken-open place and to be God there. The practice of lament has been described as the most profound demonstration of trust in a loving God because it demonstrates an unwillingness to let go of God no matter how awful the situation. Lament is the opposite of despair, which gives up on hope that something can be done, that believes that God is uninvolved and cannot be reached. Lament hooks into God with hope and desperation and trust – and hangs on. And it is worship. This form of worship, this offering up of our pain, honours God because it brings all that we are in the muddled mess of our lives, and places it as an offering before God.

How long, O Lord?

Perhaps what is so impressive and also so challenging about Habakkuk in his situation is that he is not stoical, resigned, rebellious or antagonistic; he is thoroughly engaged with God, honest and open with all that he is with a God he so obviously trusts. His entrance into lament explodes with the words, 'How long, O Lord' (Habakkuk 1:2). His anguished question is focused on the corruption at the heart of the national life of Israel, and so he brings to God a list of the awfulness that he is witnessing daily: violence, injustice, abuse, corruption and conflict (Habakkuk 1:3–4). And he's had enough. He is worn out with the exploitation that is rampant among political and religious leaders. He is worn out too with telling God all about it and receiving no response. Nowhere does he display any doubt that God is able to intervene, that God is able to judge and discipline and restore his errant people. God's power is not in question here; it's God's seeming tolerance of it all that is so deeply distressing to him.

There are times when we watch the evening news and we know exactly how Habakkuk is feeling here. His description of Israelite society at this time is not a million miles from what we view on our TV screens, from what we experience in our lives. The corruption and sordidness of the lives of some political leaders, the mismanagement of institutional funds, the seemingly unchallenged and capricious injustices at national and international level, which result in so much misery and hurt for so many vulnerable people, the salacious reporting of the scandals of celebrities – these can leave us feeling stained and drained after 20 minutes of such exposure, and we may find ourselves standing in frustrated solidarity with Habakkuk and asking God the same question: 'How long is this going to go on for?'

But it's not just other lives, lived in other places, which evoke this response in us; we have our own questions for God. So many of us have whispered – or shouted – exactly the same words from the bottom of the shadowed valleys of our own bewildering circumstances, from within the aching depths of our own personal misery. We may identify with David's pleading question as he faces the long absence of God's presence in his life: 'O Lord, how long will you forget me? Forever?' (Psalm 13:1). Or, as he continues, 'How long must I struggle with anguish in my soul, with sorrow in my heart every day?' (v. 2). So often in the book of Psalms, we see the psalmists hanging on to God with their questions. These question marks became grappling hooks with which they dug into the rock of God in their distress with life, with their circumstances, even with God himself. In Psalm 35:17 David asks, 'How long, O Lord, will you look on and do nothing?' In Psalm 6:3 he prays, 'I am sick at heart. How long, O Lord, until you restore me?'

And the probability is, if we live long enough, that question will be found on our own lips:

How long before I wake up at the start of a day and not dread facing what the day holds?
How long before this pain eases?
How long before this relationship heals?
How long before this makes any sense?
How long…?

Perhaps the hardest part to handle in such a prayer is the open-endedness of the wait before the question is answered in any way that makes sense to us. If we just had an end in sight, if we just had some idea of whether we needed to hang on for a month, or two months, or a year before God answered and brought some kind of resolution to our question, then we could probably muster up the patience, the endurance necessary to wait. But honestly confronting this seeming non-responsiveness of God draws us inexorably to diverging paths: one path leads us to a deeper place of trust, the other into a place of hopeless despair or desperate action. We can allow our experience to turn us toward the truth of the unfathomable mystery of the goodness of God, or toward a narrative of abandonment and indifference that our circumstances may be weaving for us. The waiting can become a crucible in which our convictions about God, about how life works, about who we are to God, become tested and refined.

O God, why?

As I read through the psalms and follow the journeys of Moses and Jeremiah and Job and even Jesus, I discover that in addition to the words 'How long', the word 'Why' also features strongly in their vocabulary when they engage honestly with God.

During the days of Jenny's treatment and then just after her death, some people warned me against asking the question, 'Why?' There was an implication that the question 'Why?' was a faithless question, and possibly a wilfully defiant question. Who was I to question God's purposes? What was the point anyway? God does whatever he pleases, and he always does what is good, so asking God 'Why?' is an inappropriate question. The inference seemed to be that it was not possible to trust and to struggle at the same time; it was not possible for doubt and discouragement to coexist with deep faith and hope. My questions might have been interpreted as disrespectful complaining – but they were not. Complaining against God to others seems to put distance between God and us. Honest lament, however, picks up our complaints and takes them to God. In lament, we engage directly with God about God and his actions in our lives.

My complaints were made face to face with the God I loved and trusted. 'Why?' was not a word of doubt, but of naked trust. It was an honest admission of my own lack of wisdom and, perhaps more, an admission that God and his ways were so beyond my understanding, that through my own thinking I couldn't even begin to fathom what was going on. My whole soul seemed stripped of any protective layers; I was bare before God, my own wisdom and understanding in tatters, my words ragged and beggared. The word 'Why?' was the empty bowl which I held out before God, day after day after day, trusting, hoping, it would be filled with answers, with reasons, with peace.

Our Bibles are littered with this word 'Why?' tumbling out of the mouths of those we recognise as heroes of faith. It was a question they lifted from their own breaking and bewildered hearts. In Numbers 11:11–15, in Eugene Peterson's robust translation, Moses asks God, 'Why are you treating me this way? What did I ever do to you to deserve this?… If this is how you intend to treat me, do me a favour and kill me. I've seen enough; I've had enough. Let me get out of here.' Over and over in the book of Job, this God-declared righteous man so often asks why: '*Why* have you made me your target?' (7:20), '*Why* do you turn away from me?' (13:24), '*Why* should I struggle in vain?' (9:29, NIV), '*Why* doesn't the Almighty bring the wicked to judgement?' (24:1), '*Why* then did you deliver me from my mother's womb?' (10:18).

Even Jesus asked 'Why?' from the depth of his cross-held agony. He asks the Father, whose love has always held him, whose presence is the bedrock of his life, 'Why have you abandoned me?' (Mark 15:34).

What is so striking as we read these scriptures, and as we explore the relationship that these question holders had with God, is that these bold questions didn't appear to faze God at all. Judging from his responses, God was not insulted, aggrieved or offended; rather, he seems to honour the integrity of the questions. It seems for example in Moses' case, that far from threatening the relationship, Moses' honesty with God seems to have strengthened their friendship. Exodus 33:11 tells us that God spoke to Moses face to face as a man speaks to his friend; God and Moses shared a friendship with each other in which they could be honest and open, in which the bridge of trust that had been built over many shared moments together could be crossed with great freedom. This same bridge of trust is one which we see the psalmists crossing many times, and it was their borrowed words which so often carried me toward the heart of God during the long months of Jenny's treatment.

Reading back through my journal entries from that time, it seems as though I lived in the psalms. Almost daily, the psalmists' words met me where I was in this tortuous journey. I would take their words and make them my own. I read the words of Psalm 10 which opens with a burst of questions, 'O Lord, *why do you stand so far away? Why do you hide when I am in trouble?*' (v. 1). And I substituted the psalmist's questions with my own: 'Why is this treatment not working? Why are the tumours not shrinking?' And I asked my own 'How long?' questions too: 'How long till she can eat again? How long till her hair grows back? How long will this pain last?' As the treatments failed, one after another, I asked, 'How long before she can die and be freed from this monster which is destroying her life?' And, like Habakkuk, for the longest time, although God seemed to speak about so much else in my life, as far as Jenny was concerned all I heard was the sound of his silence. And my questions continued to jab into my prayers, unrelenting and unanswered.

During this time, while leading a retreat in Northern Ireland, one of the women attending read out words by the writer Susan Lenzkes. In those words, I heard God's reassurance to me that he was more than able to hold the jagged brokenness of my heart and all the ways that brokenness expressed itself:

> *It's all right –*
> *questions, pain,*
> *and stabbing anger,*
> *can be poured out to*
> *the Infinite One and*
> *he will not be damaged.*
> *Our wounded raging will be*
> *lost in him and*
> *we*
> *   will*
> *   be*
> *found.*
> *For we beat on his chest*
> *from within*
> *the circle of his arms.*[7]

I believe that Habakkuk knew the circle of those arms. I believe he knew the strong embrace of the God who would not, ever, let him go. The opening words of his prophecy may be bursting with frustration and bafflement, but they are addressed to God directly. He speaks as a man safe.

The God of loving presence

To be as honest with God as Habakkuk was, and to speak the language of lament so fluently, demands that we know and trust the God whom he consistently addresses as Yahweh, the God of loving presence, who will never walk off and leave us, who will never abandon us out of exasperation or frustration. The Amplified Bible's translation of Hebrews 13:5 is one I memorised as a new believer and which I clung to so often and so tightly during Jenny's cancer treatments. In this verse God declares, 'I will not in any way fail you *nor* give you up *nor* leave you without support… [I will] not in any degree leave you helpless *nor* forsake *nor* let [you] down (relax My hold on you)!' To worship God in the words of our lament is to acknowledge that at the core of my relationship with God is not my love of him but his unchanging, passionate, committed love for me. My soul may barely cling to him, but his hand holds me tight. I may not be able to make any sense of his actions – or non-actions – but I can trust the love of his heart for me and for those I love. Our laments are actually defiant acts of faith and worship which acknowledge the truth of God's loving kindness in our lives, however hidden that loving kindness may be in our present circumstances.

Over many years, I have learned that unless we know ourselves to be safe in the unchanging love of the One we worship, we may fear offending God with the words of our lament; we may fear losing his favour and approval, we may fear his judgement and punishment. We may fear God in ways that are neither holy nor wholesome, nor biblical. To be as vulnerably honest as Habakkuk or Moses or Job or David assumes a depth of trust in a God who is unshakeably committed to both the integrity of his character and to the welfare of his children.

There may be some who look at these broken men in the raw desperation of their distraught outpourings to God, and assume that the Holy Spirit's witness captures them in weakness and disbelief. Viewed from such a perspective, these men are compromising their faith, disrespecting God, and in those 'caught on camera' moments, they are examples to us of how *not* to relate to God. But I see in their responses to God's dealings in their lives an affirmation of their deep-seated understanding that God cannot be shocked into an aggrieved retaliatory response out of a fit of pique. The absolutely stable, righteous kindness of God can hold steady in the face of all that may be confused and unbalanced in our lives, even when expressed in words which are uncensored and unfiltered. We forget so often that God knows the secrets of every heart, he knows our thoughts and the intentions of our hearts and, in whatever fine words we may dress up our prayers to God, those words cannot disguise the truth of what he already sees and knows and understands.

C.S. Lewis wrote that 'we should bring to God what is in us, not what ought to be in us'.[8] Ken Gire, commenting on these words, writes, 'The "oughts" will keep us from telling the truth. They will also keep us from feeling the truth. Especially the truth about our pain.' Reflecting on Jesus' experience in Gethsemane, he continues, 'We pray however we can, with whatever words we can. We pray with our sweat, with our tears. And with whatever friends we have who will sit with us in the darkness.'[9]

As we read the accounts of lament in our Bibles, one thing becomes so clear: our laments do not leave God untouched, no matter how it may appear otherwise. In verse 3 in *THE MESSAGE* version of this opening chapter of his prophesy, Habakkuk tells God that 'day after day' he has waited and called for help in the face of God's silence. Peterson's translation captures the frustration of the waiting – 'How many times do I have to yell… before you come to the rescue?' He has waited for some word from God that would indicate that God is aware of what is going on. And then it happens: God answers! He responds to Habakkuk's prayers with a staggering revelation. God basically tells Habakkuk, 'You need to know that I am not inactive, I am not inattentive and I am not indolent. I am working. But you are not going to believe what I am going to do!' Habakkuk didn't.

Practice: Write your own prayer of lament

In prayer, we need to speak whatever truth is in us; pain and grief, fear and disappointment, yearning and desire, questions and doubt, hope and faith, failure and weakness, praise and thanks, despair and sorrow, anger, and yes, even hatred.[10]

The honest outpouring of Habakkuk's heart to God gives us an insight into the heart of prayer and into the practice of lament. I wonder if Habakkuk learned to pray like this by soaking his heart in the psalms of lament with which he would have been so familiar? Trusting in God's love, power, understanding and forgiveness, the psalmists poured out their words to God. Their prayers were wrung from the reality of their tragedies, their shattered dreams, their broken hopes. They prayed with raw honesty, with uncensored candour.

Writing our own prayer or psalm of lament may be a way of recognising more clearly what is really going on inside us when we are bewildered or distressed by God's actions or non-actions in our lives. We may have stuffed the pockets of our hearts with rage, fear, hopelessness, despair, desires and a welter of other emotions, and those pockets may need emptying in God's presence. Facing and owning these emotions and then expressing them as honestly as we can to God may clear a space for God to be present with us in the place of our own struggling. As we experience God in that space, we may find like the psalmists before us that his presence brings perspective and release and peace and the possibility of transformation *within* us, even if the circumstances around us don't change.

Steps into your own psalm of lament

The psalms of lament testify to the reality of the psalmists' lives and their confidence in God as they bring those lives in all their complexity, to God in prayer. They are the unvarnished, honest outpourings of hurting hearts. And this is where we begin writing our own psalm; with an honest expression of what is true for us right here, right now. As you write your own psalm, know that God understands the depths of where you are, and he is inviting you, through this writing, to pour out your heart to him.

- Begin by identifying a relationship, or a situation, or a set of circumstances which has been or may still be churning up your peace and unsettling your soul right now. As fully as you can, write out a description of what is troubling you, including the emotions that are part of that.

- How are you experiencing God in all of this? Is God present, absent, uninvolved, caring, concerned? Who is God for you in all of this? Again, as fully as you can, write out your responses to these questions.

- Now look at what you've written and highlight any words or phrases which especially capture what you would want to say to God.

- When you are ready, write your prayer of lament beginning perhaps with the words 'Lord' (or whatever name for God that is most comfortable or real for you right now), 'I need to tell you something…' and go on from there, pouring out in words, the truth of your life right now. Don't edit, just write.

- Apart from just one psalm, Psalm 88, the psalms of lament end with a declaration of praise, of thankfulness for the truth of God's character – his love, mercy, justice, compassion and so on. As you finish your own psalm of lament, and as an act of hopeful trust, you might want to write a sentence or two which reflects something of what you believe is true about God.

- When you've finished writing, you might want to pray your psalm out loud to God as an act of worship.

The psalms were not just the prayer book of the Old Testament, but also the songbook of God's people, so you might want to consider putting the words of your psalm to music, or if you are more comfortable, try expressing the substance of your psalm through a painting or a drawing or a sculpture.

Chapter 3

It wasn't meant to be like this

Living by faith is a bewildering venture. We rarely know what's coming next, and not many things turn out the way we anticipate.
Eugene Peterson[11]

Look long and hard. Brace yourself for a shock.
HABAKKUK 1:5 (*The Message*)

As he sets to answering Habakkuk's complaints, it is obvious that God is aware that he is about to blow Habakkuk's mind. Far from being inattentive and inactive or indolent, God has actually been preparing for Judah's long-term restoration – at the hands of the Babylonians.

To understand the stunning shock that this would have been to Habakkuk, we need to understand that, in Habakkuk's day, the Babylonians had a reputation for terror and barbarism. They were known to be wicked, ruthless, cruel. They were fierce in battle, totally dominating their opponents and, once conquered, the prisoners of war they took were subject to unimaginable torture. God himself describes them to Habakkuk as 'fierce and ferocious… dreadful and terrible… vultures circling in on carrion' (1:5–8, *The Message*). They were in every single sense Judah's enemy. And yet this very nation was God's chosen instrument of redemptive discipline and eventual restoration for Judah. God was going to use a nation which, in Habakkuk's eyes, was so much worse than Judah to judge her wickedness. It was unthinkable. It would be the equivalent of today's most feared terrorists being given free rein in the streets of our cities to wreak whatever destruction and death they wanted to with the full permission of God. It would be an unbelievable act of unimaginable wickedness. And yet this is what seems to be happening here.

In Habakkuk's limited and human thinking, there was only one solution to the problem that Judah had – she needed rescuing and God was the one to do it. There was good precedent for this confidence: God had done it before. The whole of the exodus history, for example, had begun with God's statement to Moses that the cry of his people had reached his ears, and he was coming down to rescue them. And he was sending Moses to effect that rescue (Exodus 3:7–10). This made sense – sort of. Moses might have been a murderer, a fugitive sheep herder on the back side of the desert, but at least he was one of God's own. This kept the rescuing in the family as it were. But this? This was a violation of everything that Habakkuk believed to be true about God's relationship with his people.

Habakkuk is described in the opening words of this book as 'the prophet' – this was his role in life. He was a man chosen by God, who was experienced in hearing and understanding, in interpreting and communicating the word of God to the people of God. It would have been very natural for him to assume that he understood how God should deal with Judah. His whole professional life revolved around engaging with God and his word. His prayers were shaped by the convictions he held about the character of God and God's purposes for his people, and so he had prayed for God to bring about renewal and revival in Judah. He probably had some kind of idea in mind of how God would go about doing that, but if his reactions to God's revelations are any indication, the difference between his ideas of good and God's idea of good was stunning.

Facing a new reality

Habakkuk's responses to God's revelation about his plans for Judah consist of flabbergasted statements in which he reels from one exclamation mark to another. In THE MESSAGE translation, his shocked responses are rendered particularly colourfully: 'You can't be serious!… Why don't you do something about this?' (1:12–13). His response was rooted in what he believed about God's involvement with his people, in God's long-standing covenant with them. He believed that there was no way that God would violate such a covenant because to do so would be to violate his own nature, his own character – and that was an impossibility. Wasn't it?

The truth was that Judah *did* need rescuing and God *was* the one to do it, but the way in which he would do it was not only out of the box, it demonstrated so clearly to Habakkuk that as far as God was concerned, there was no box. And it began to dawn on Habakkuk that his God was dependable, but not necessarily predictable. He seems totally overwhelmed, totally bewildered by the actions which God is planning. There is a tender poignancy in the words he uses to address God: 'O LORD my God… O LORD, our Rock…' (1:12). His confusion is palpable and you can almost hear the agonised protestation, yelled through the megaphone of his distress: 'It wasn't meant to be like this.'

These words intruded into the days of Jenny's treatment and death. Cancer happened to other people, to other families, not to ours. The death of a child was something we read about in women's magazines flicked through as we waited in the doctor's surgery or the dentist or the tyre shop; it happened out there, wherever 'there' was, but it wasn't meant to happen here, in *our* family. Jenny was meant to graduate from university, establish herself in her chosen career of social work, eventually meet a man special enough for her, marriage, children and, as the years passed, grandchildren and, eventually, at the end of a long and rich life, death. This savagely edited version was not how it was meant to be.

We each have our own cover version of this theme song: a disappointing marriage, troubled children, a job which seems to be going nowhere, a longed-for relationship which never happened, long-term unemployment, chronic sickness, retirement savings which no longer cover retirement expenses, the unrelieved boredom and loneliness of the same day repeated over and over and over again, with only memories and dreams for companions. It may be nothing too dramatic, just the gradual erosion of our hopes and longings, the quiet accumulation of disappointments scattered across the landscape of our lives. And we may whisper in the shadowed greyness of those days, 'It wasn't meant to be like this.'

I wonder if those words ever crossed the mind of God on that sad evening when he discovered that his beloved creation masterpieces had just traded paradise for a piece of fruit. I wonder if, as he looked into Eve's eyes that evening, he saw there not the innocence of the morning, but the knowing look of guilt and shame which the day's encounter with evil had brought. I wonder if God the Father sighed those words to himself even as he turned to his Son and the Spirit with the knowledge of what must now be put in motion, a plan which Paul tells us had been in the heart and mind of God since before the creation of the world,[12] a plan which would come to fulfilment in another garden and on another hill one day. I wonder.

The writer of the book of Hebrews tells us that in Jesus we do not have a high priest who is out of touch with our reality, or one for whom our weaknesses are unintelligible; we have a God who knows disappointment and bewilderment and aching gut-wrenching despair from the *inside* of our humanity (Hebrews 4:15). The theologian Nicholas Wolterstorff, writing about the tragic death of his 25-year-old son in a climbing accident, wrote, 'God is not only the God of the sufferers but the God who suffers. The pain and fallenness of humanity have entered into his heart. Through the prism of my tears I have seen a suffering God.'[13] And I wonder if that same God looks through the prism of *his own* tears – and sees us?

Over time, we may find ourselves standing with so many other dazed and disappointed men and women who daily wake up to the reality that this is not how they imagined their lives would turn out, how their lives were meant to be. If God had been brought into these broken expectations through prayer, and if that same God had not answered those prayers in anticipated ways, then the dread awfulness of that phrase is even more acute. Psalm 62:8 encourages us to pour out our hearts to God, freely and with abandon. It assures us that God listens to our prayers with total attention. What it does not guarantee is an answer that slots neatly into the space we have left for it in the jigsaw puzzle of our own limited understanding.

Letting go

Some time ago, one of my students told me the (surely apocryphal) story of a man who got stuck on the roof of his house as the floodwaters rose around him. As the waters rose, he moved further and further up the house, praying all the while that God would rescue him, claiming God's promise from Isaiah 43:2 that the floodwaters would not overwhelm him. During that time, a rescue boat came for him, but he sent it away, telling them that he was waiting for God to rescue him. Other boats came and went. Finally, he ended up on the roof, whereupon a helicopter appeared and a winchman was lowered down to pick him up. But he turned down the offer of help, tenaciously clinging on to a chimney pot and the hope that God would rescue him. When he eventually drowned and appeared before God in heaven, he was not a happy man. Talking with God, he complained loudly that he had prayed for God to answer him and God had chosen to let him drown. After listening for a while, God finally interrupted his foolishness: 'I sent a boat and I sent a helicopter; you turned them down. What more could I have done?'

He was so entrenched in how he believed God would answer his prayers that it cost him his life. In order to be saved, he needed not only to let go of the chimney pot but also his ideas of how God would answer his prayers, how God would fulfil his promise, how God would be God for him in that situation. His tenacious unwillingness to believe that God could behave in any way that would contradict his understanding of how God should act may be amusing, but it was also life-threatening.

This willingness to allow God to act differently from his expectations was going to be Habakkuk's challenge as he came to terms with God's revelation to him. It wouldn't be an easy shift to make in his thinking and it's not an easy shift to make in our own. To move from our expectations of how God should act to the reality of the present actions of God is never easy. It demands a willingness to let go; just as a trapeze artist hangs suspended in the air between the bar he's let go of, trusting that the swinging bar will reach him in time, so letting go of our expectations of God and trusting that God might be even greater, even bigger, than we've experienced is a challenging place to be in. I think this might have been the challenge that Habakkuk faced in his shocking exchange with God that day: the challenge to let go of his expectations of how God should respond and act. To let God be God, even when that image of God didn't match what he had come to believe.

I think this is the same challenge we face almost daily, this willingness to allow God to be and to act in ways that are consistent with the fullest dimensions of his character and purposes, even when we don't understand or agree with the changes we are being presented with. Letting go of our dearly held convictions about God's character in the face of new and perhaps contradictory revelations of that character can be so very disorienting, deeply unsettling and, at times, as scary as letting go of a chimney pot in a flood.

For some of us, we may need to let go of the picture we have of God as the uncaring boss who pushes us to work harder and harder and who is disappointed when we are not productive. Some of us may have an entrenched image of God as an absent parent, who provides for us, who plans for us, but who is never at home, never truly available, so we never really trust the relationship. Some of us may need to let go of an image of God as a traffic policeman, coming up behind us, watching every move and just waiting for us to get something wrong so he can slap some kind of punishment on us. If our image of God does not look like Jesus, who is the exact image of God, then we probably don't have an accurate image of God, no matter how long we have held it, no matter how often it has been reinforced by others. If our image of God doesn't line up with the portrayal that we have of the Lord Jesus in the Gospels, it's not God. Many of us have developed understandings or images of God that we have clung to for many years and God may be wanting to move us into new and fresh and expanded understandings of who he is. This move is important because clinging to an inadequate or incomplete understanding of God shapes our responses to his unexpected actions in our lives.

In his book *Reaching for the Invisible God*, Philip Yancey writes that there seem to be two major responses to God's dealings with us: 'if… then' or 'even though… nevertheless'.[14] We see Habakkuk's 'even though… nevertheless' at the end of his prophesy, but in the conversation recorded for us here in 1:12–17, he hasn't reached that part of the journey yet. In this encounter with God, he is still clinging to the 'if… then' pattern of his past. He seems to be faced with letting go of his dearly held assumptions that:

- If God is a rock, then he cannot change who he has always been.
- If God is a God of covenant kindness, then there is no way that he can compromise that covenant by treating Judah harshly.
- If God is righteous, then he cannot use a people less righteous than his own people to deal with Judah.

Earlier, I wrote of my own letting go the night before Jenny's funeral. Of how in those quiet moments I let go of blaming God, of his needing to work out this awfulness 'together for good' for my life and the life of my family. This letting go was a significant step of relinquishment for me, a needed step clearing space for the new and transformative growth that God was purposing for me. There are other lettings go in our lives that are no less transformative:

- The challenge to let go of old ways of being or of doing things, of being willing to try new things, to take new risks with how we do life, relationships, ministry or work.
- Letting go of a past we cannot change, letting go of guilt and shame, the burden of the consequences of unwise decisions, of hurt or regret that may have shaped that past.
- The challenge of letting go of our reputation or our image or of defending ourselves when that reputation is threatened.
- Letting go of grievances and the 'right' to bear grudges; letting go of nursing unforgiveness, the desire for revenge.
- The need to let go of our idea of justice, of fairness, of good outcomes to our prayers.
- The need to let go of the memory of that sin which we have confessed, which we have repented of over and over again, but like Velcro, the memory sticks to our soul.

If we are holding too tightly to what we believe God should or could be doing, then we will probably not experience the peace that eventually accompanies this releasing. As we let go, we discover a new freedom to move on to what could be God's next step for us. This act of letting go is an act of courage in the face of our fears of the unknown, our fears of losing control, our fears of losing ourselves. My experience has been that letting go in this profound way seems to happen over time: through tiny movements of release and surrender, seeded in quiet space alone with God. And it's this needed time and space that we see Habakkuk embracing in the next movement of this journey.

In the midst of his confusion and despair and anguish, Habakkuk does something very wise: he stops. He doesn't go any further. He doesn't argue any more with God. He just stops. What he has heard about the purposes of God has been traumatic, and he doesn't minimise this trauma with a 'business as usual' approach to life. Bearing the burden of this revelation from God would have been crushing – emotionally and spiritually – and he would probably have been weary, discouraged, bewildered, achingly confused – and this is not the time to make decisions, judgements or pronouncements. So, wisely, he stops; he deliberately and very decisively removes himself from the immediacy of the situation and places himself in a position to listen to God. In 2:1, we read that he climbs into a high tower and in that place he 'will wait to see what Lord says'.

Habakkuk knew God well enough to believe that what he had heard wasn't God's last word on the subject. There was more to come – and he trusted that, as he withdrew and as he waited, more would be revealed.

When our own journey with God brings us to this place of stunned reality, when all the words we know to say have been said, all we know to do done, all the prayers prayed, I wonder if the wisest course of action is not to go forward, but to stop, to honour our confusion and our hurt not with more words, but with silence; not with frenetic activity, which tries to run away from the reality we are confronted with, but with intentional stillness. To sit with our hurt and our pain in the presence of the God who knows all there is to know of that pain, to the very depth of it. I wonder if we sometimes miss God's soothing of our hearts when we rush into whatever we believe will ease the pain, still the turmoil, soften the blow of what we are learning about God, about ourselves, about life and how it is unfolding for us. I wonder if we sometimes miss how God might want to minister to us because we are too eager to move on, too quick to relieve the ache we feel with the analgesic of activity, and because of that we sink into despair and into hopelessness, and sooner or later perhaps, a withdrawal from the very presence of the God of all comfort.

Habakkuk stopped; he quit pouring out his own words to God, and placed himself in a position to listen for fresh words from God. In doing this, he relinquished his grip on what might have been, and placed himself in a position to receive from God the revelation of what was yet to be. And it would be a revelation which would not only change Habakkuk's life, but in time, ours as well.

Practice:
Steps into the prayer of relinquishment

At the beginning of chapter 2, we see Habakkuk climbing up into one of the watchtowers on the city walls, where he determines to wait for God to answer his questions, to address the turmoil in his heart. He had been struggling so much with God's revelation, with the awfulness of the words he'd heard from God. His move to the watchtower is a decisive withdrawal from the struggle he is experiencing. He is intentionally moving into a place of letting go, of releasing his hold on his own will and desires. This is not an act of resignation or defeat; it is an act of relinquishment of his own ways, and a desire to understand and embrace God's ways.

The words 'abandonment', 'sacrifice', 'renunciation' and 'release' are just a sampling of the synonyms for the word 'relinquishment' offered by the dictionary programme on my computer. They are strong words. Hard to swallow words. But they are also words of transformation and invitation, of freedom and hope as we follow them through to their end – the hands and heart of a loving and tender God who longs for our best, and who waits for us to be willing to receive it through the pathway of relinquishment. The prayer of relinquishment was one I prayed many, many times during Jenny's treatment and after her death. It is a prayer I am still praying.

At its heart, this prayer follows in the footsteps of Jesus, and echoes the intent of his words: 'Not my will, but yours be done' (Luke 22:42, NIV).

Praying the prayer

When you are ready to begin this prayer, you might want to close your eyes and picture the open hands of God before you. Now open your own hands and as you do, bring to mind the people and relationships in your life; your concerns for them, any anxieties or fears you may have over them, your dreams and desires for them.

Picture them held in your open hands. Now, turn your hands over, palms down, and one by one, drop those things you are holding into God's hands. As you do this, entrust them to the Lord with the words, 'Father, I release _____ into your hands; thank you that you will hold them in your love', or similar. Then turn your hands palm-side up again with the prayer, 'Father, I receive from you _____.' Allow God to bring whatever word or image he chooses to give you at this moment. Don't rush this time. Then, when you are ready, thank him for what he has taken and for whatever he has given to you.

Next, bring to mind your own heart's dreams, desires, hopes, fears and frustrations, your longing for God and any struggles you may have with him over what may be going on in your life. Bring to mind any need or desire you may have to control your life and perhaps the lives of those you love. If there are patterns of behaving or believing that you sense may not be healthy or helpful for you at this time and that you need to let go of, bring them too. Hold them in your upturned hands, and name them before God as fully as you can. Then again, turning your hands over, drop them one by one into the hands of God with words of surrender or release and thankfulness, and then again, turn your hands over once more to receive from him.

Then, if you are able, hold in your hands any grievances you may have with God or others, any regrets, any quarrel with anyone, any desire for revenge or retaliation. Hold them in your hands and then, again, turn them over and drop them into the waiting hands of God with whatever words of surrender, release and thankfulness you have, and again turn up your open hands to receive.

Finally, close this prayer time with your open hands resting in your lap as an external sign of your heart's attitude to go into the rest of your day and all it holds, open to the presence of God in and through the day.

The prayer of relinquishment offers so many rewards and perhaps the biggest reward is freedom – freedom from the tyranny of our own demanding natures. Freedom from our own fears, our own control, from the cost of our own misguided wisdom. But also freedom to embrace a new way of being and doing, of believing and acting. There is so much freedom to be gained when we empty our hands of all that we are grasping so tightly out of fear or other needs, and opening our hands to all that God would want to place in them now that they are free to receive.

Chapter 4

Don't just do something, sit there!

I will climb up to my watchtower
 and stand at my guard post.
There I will wait to see what the Lord says
 and how he will answer my complaint.
HABAKKUK 2:1

When life is heavy and hard to take,
 go off by yourself. Enter the silence.
Bow in prayer. Don't ask questions;
 wait for hope to appear.
LAMENTATIONS 3:28–29 (*THE MESSAGE*)

Jeremiah's words, birthed in wisdom from the womb of his own lamentation over the destruction of Jerusalem, are words of practical, sound advice for our own lives when we find ourselves in distressing and bewildering circumstances. The natural response in those circumstances is to turn to those who will comfort, encourage and strengthen us. And so many times this is appropriate and wise and helpful to do. But those to whom we turn cannot be for us what only God can be. He is the one who knows the ache of our hearts; he *knows* us – and he knows too the words that our hearts need to hear from him, words that we miss so often by turning too quickly to the words of others.

Through the months of Jenny's worsening condition and after her death, I had been so very well and tenderly supported by the loving and compassionate words of so many of my friends and colleagues and prayer partners. Their words had supported me on many days when I thought I would fall into a deep hole and never emerge again.

On that bleak evening before Jenny's funeral, however, I found myself echoing Peter's words to Jesus by saying, 'Lord, I have no one else to go to; you *alone* have the words which can heal me and free me; I choose you.' In the months that followed, I prayed and sobbed and whispered those same words; 'I choose you; I choose you' – words which cradled trust and hope that his life-giving word would reach the very depths of where I was and transform me there.

There are times in our lives when we are desperately, acutely aware that only *God's* words will do and, in those times, we need to take Jeremiah's words seriously; we need intentionally to take ourselves off to whatever space helps us to engage with God and his word without distraction; we need to bow in prayer, and we need to wait for hope to reappear. It is exactly this that we witness Habakkuk doing at the beginning of chapter 2.

A time to listen

My guess is that when Habakkuk withdrew to the watchtower, he was a broken man; my guess is that he was shaken to the core by what God had told him about what was going to happen. He *believed* what God had told him – and it was awful. He had prayed honest and God-honouring prayers, and God had shown him that what he had prayed and hoped for was not going to happen in the way Habakkuk had wanted. Disappointment, despair, confusion – I wonder at what depths he was experiencing these emotions. It would have been so easy to have just let go; to have just gone with the flow of his feelings, to have surrendered to the circumstances with hopelessness, to have sunk into a numb apathy. He had enough cause: unanswered prayer, a God he had served but hardly seemed to recognise anymore, a country tailspinning out of control, enemies within and without the city gates. But he didn't go there. He put the brakes on his emotions and the place they could have taken him and he stopped, and he waited for God to speak to him.

In the midst of his discouragement, confusion and weariness, he recognised that this was not the time for action; it was the time to stop. It was not a time for words, but a time for silence, a time for listening. And so, in contrast to the torrent of words of the previous chapter, Habakkuk enters the watchtower with no words of advice for God on how he should handle the situation. He asks no more questions; he makes no requests. Instead, he waits, and this silent waiting is fragrant with hope. 'I will wait to see *what* the Lord says' – not *if* he will say anything.

When Habakkuk climbed into that tower, he did so with a clear expectation that God would speak to him. In his role as prophet he had experienced hearing and recognising the voice of God, and his actions here demonstrate the conviction that he would hear that voice again speaking into the hopelessness of his situation, into the breaking of his heart. Habakkuk expects that God will speak to him if only he waits. We have no idea how long he sat there in the watchtower; no idea how many long, lonely nights he spent, craning for the whisper of a word from God. We have no idea of how long it was before God spoke to him; all we know is that God did show up, and he did respond to Habakkuk's surrendered withdrawal with new revelations of his purpose for his people.

In that time of silent withdrawal, Habakkuk heard words that would change his world – and our world too. He heard God say, 'the righteous live by their faith' (2:4, NRSV). Six hundred years later, the apostle Paul would use these very words in his letter to the church in Rome, and almost 1,500 years after this, a troubled and guilt-ridden monk named Martin Luther, reading those same words in that letter to the Romans, would enter into a new understanding of salvation and grace, and out of that new and life-changing understanding, the Protestant Reformation was born, and the world itself was changed! And all this happened because one bewildered, hurting, lonely man of God made the decision to stop, to withdraw, to listen to God and obediently to write down what he heard.

Habakkuk could never have imagined how his journey with God, his honesty and integrity, his anguished laments, would end up shaping the faith of literally millions of men and women down through the centuries. And neither do we know the impact that our encounters with God have on the world. We have no idea of how wide the ripples of our honest and authentic engagement with God may spread throughout the world, so when we are hurting, bewildered, disappointed and dismayed, instead of withdrawing *from* God, we can follow Habakkuk and countless others in a trusting act of withdrawing *with* God, and *to* God.

This act of withdrawing for a while from the pressing demands both around us and within us in order to more intentionally care for the needs of our battered souls has a solid track record among God's people. Moses often withdrew from the daunting demands of his desert journey to meet with God in the Tent of Meeting (Exodus 33:7). The psalmist tells us in Psalm 73 that his jealousy and anger over the prosperity of the wicked was put into perspective as he met with God; he writes: 'Then I went into your sanctuary O God and I finally understood the destiny of the wicked... I realised that my heart was bitter, and I was all torn up inside' (vv. 17, 21). He gained a perspective on his circumstances and the state of his soul that would have been lost to him had he not withdrawn to be with God, if he had pursued a 'business as usual' mode. And then there's Jesus, whom Luke tells us 'often withdrew to the wilderness for prayer' (Luke 5:16); to recalibrate his direction, to gain his father's perspective on his life and his purpose, and to soak himself in his father's love. Out of those times of withdrawal came a sure-footed, purpose-laden walk on his path to the cross, a peace which held him through days of rejection and misunderstandings, a joy that was expansive enough to overflow into the lives of others and a grace-touched wisdom that shaped his words and actions. So much of the wonder of Jesus' life and ministry flowed out of those times of withdrawal, and it can be the same for us as we follow in his footsteps.

David advises us in Psalm 37:7 to 'be still in the presence of the Lord, and wait patiently for him to act'. And in Psalm 40:1 the psalmist encourages us that this waiting is worth it. He writes, 'I waited patiently for the Lord to help me, and he turned to me and heard my cry.' Sometimes that's all we need from God; just the assurance that our cry has been heard; that God has turned his kind face toward us, and our distress is known and understood. Sometimes though we cry to God, but then walk away into the next thing before we ever experience the comfort that he is waiting to give us. Sometimes we just don't wait long enough, perhaps, or underlying this may be the truth that we don't actually believe or trust that a quiet waiting with God, for God, will actually change anything. But the testimony of the people of God down through the centuries gives the lie to this thinking; they would wholeheartedly say, 'God is worth the wait!'

Just wait

The word 'wait' is an important biblical word; it appears over 100 times in the scriptures and most of those references relate to waiting for God. Our patient waiting seems to allow God the opportunity to act, to respond, to speak, to renew our perspective, to restore courage, to rebuild hope in our hearts for the journey, to transform our lives and fulfil his purposes. So much happens *in* the waiting, *through* the waiting, so it's perhaps not surprising that this theme of waiting seems to thread its way through the lives of the men and women who inhabit the pages of our Bibles. We watch Abraham waiting 25 years for the fulfilment of the promise of God to give him a son; we stand on tiptoe with the children of Israel waiting to enter the promised land. We see Joseph waiting for his amazing dreams to come true, David waiting 20 years for his throne, Hannah waiting for the answer to her prayers for a child. At the very beginning of the New Testament, we see Anna and Simeon waiting for the word of God to be fulfilled to them in the birth of Jesus; we see Paul waiting in the desert of Arabia before beginning his ministry – and on and on till we get to the book of Revelation and discover that we ourselves are also waiting for Jesus to return and for the new heavens and earth to be revealed and received. So, we take our place with the many men and women in scripture who discovered that hopeful waiting resulted, eventually, in the realisation of God's richest purposes in their lives. As we track their journeys, we discover that wherever their waiting took them, however long the wait lasted, they themselves were transformed through the process of waiting.

Adele Ahlberg Calhoun describes waiting as 'the crucible of transformation.'[15] In the natural world, perhaps our clearest picture of this transformation through waiting is seen in the metamorphosis of the caterpillar into a butterfly or a moth. The context for the transformation is the cocoon, an enclosed space of literally suspended waiting. From the outside, nothing seems to be happening. If we were to look at the dull brown cocoon hanging on a branch, we would not be able to discern any life there, any movement, any change. But something *is* happening in this time of dark waiting. Deep within the very structure of the caterpillar, its life is being transformed. All it was ever created to be is being brought to life in that quiet waiting time. When it emerges from the cocoon, it is no longer an earth-bound creature; it has wings and magnificent colours, and it is free for the skies and the flowers. It is truly transformed. We are no less transformed in our own places of waiting; perhaps not as radically as the caterpillar, but it is no less real as we surrender to the working of God in our lives in those times.

Waiting and trusting demand that we not rush into decisions, into actions which satisfy our need to *do* something, *anything*, in order to relieve the discomfort and the distress of the situation we are in. The Nike ad tells us to 'Just do it', and we have heard others say, 'Don't just sit there, do something!' But the example of godly men and women, in scripture and in life is that there are times in our lives when the wisest advice to follow is, 'Don't just do something, sit there!'

In our ordinary everyday lives, we are aware that waiting is actually a fact of life from which there is no escape. If we live, we wait. As

I write, I have friends who are waiting for jobs, waiting to hear about test results from a brain scan, waiting to hear if their offer on a house has been accepted and if the mortgage really will come through. Others are waiting expectantly for their first child, a couple of my friends are waiting for marriage proposals, and others are waiting for the day that they finally draw their pensions. In these commonplace circumstances, there is no 'something' to do; we just have to sit, either physically or metaphorically, and wait. And we have a choice – we can either sit patiently, or fretfully; but we will sit and we will wait.

It may be obvious, but waiting demands patience – but patient waiting is actually a counter-cultural act. We live in a culture which is shaped by the expectation of the immediate and instant. In such a culture, waiting patiently for anything, even for our computers to start up, can be a frustrating experience. We have become programmed for the instant and yet very few things that last are produced in an instant. There is an element of slow time in anything worthwhile – whether it's a good stew or a good relationship. And waiting involves the willingness to take whatever time it takes for whatever it is that God wants to reveal to us, to shape in us or in the lives of those we love and care about. Such waiting invites us into the landscape of trust and hope. We have to trust that the time spent waiting, the time of seeming inactivity, is worth it. We have to trust that the healing, the restoration of hope, the rebuilding of trust or whatever it is that we so long to see and which only God can accomplish for us, will take place as we wait patiently with God, for God, to act.

THE MESSAGE translation of Romans 8:24–25 is a helpful and hopeful corrective to our more fretful, impatient waiting:

> Waiting does not diminish us, any more than waiting diminishes a pregnant mother. We are enlarged in the waiting. We, of course, don't see what is enlarging us. But the longer we wait, the larger we become, and the more joyful our expectancy.

We have no spiritual ultrasound scan to help us see what God is doing within us as we wait, but we can be sure that something transformative *is* happening; something is being formed within by God's Spirit which will eventually be brought to life in us and perhaps through us too.

Waiting may require patience, but it is not to be confused with passivity. One of the most common uses of the word 'patient' in the New Testament is rooted in the Greek word *hupomeno*, which has the connotation of bearing with, of actively enduring something until that endurance eventually produces something worthwhile. Waiting on God in the places of our brokenness and confusion and distress is an intensely active posture which holds hope in place. In fact, in Hebrew, the words 'wait' and 'hope' are often interchangeable, so in Isaiah 40:31 in the NIV, we read that those 'who hope in the Lord will renew their strength', but another translation has 'those who wait for the Lord…' (for example, NRSV). So we wait and hope with the kind of anticipation the night watchman of Psalm 130:5–6 feels as he waits for the morning sun to signal the end of his watch. No matter how many hours of darkness he has to wait through, the watchman knows from experience that morning will come. He is alert to the dangers of the night while every fibre of his being leans toward that coming dawn. His eyes have become practised in recognising any movement across the landscape outside the city walls, his heart practised at recognising the first ray of sunlight on the horizon.

This is how we are invited to wait for God – with longing, with expectancy, with alert awareness: our whole self straining to catch the earliest possible glimpse of this God who is guaranteed to come to us as surely as the dawn comes each morning, and with his coming brings hope and explosive possibilities of transformation.

I really enjoy watching films and shortly after it was released I watched the film *The Exotic Marigold Hotel*, which tells the story of a group of older men and women who for different reasons have been drawn to leave their mundane lives in the UK for the promise of a new life in a retirement community in India, based at the

Exotic Marigold Hotel. On their arrival in India, however, they are greeted not with the sight of an exotic hotel, but with the reality of a crumbling ruin, supported by temporary structures and rooms with no doors but many squatters in the shape of birds and rats. It is a magical movie, as profoundly moving as it is funny, and scattered throughout the movie are lines that stay with you long after the credits have rolled. For me, watching the movie not too long after Jenny died, the most memorable line was, 'It will be alright in the end; and if it's not alright, it's not the end.'

This line was repeated like a mantra by the young and enthusiastically inept manager of the hotel in those times when everything seemed to be going wrong, when all his plans were falling apart and there seemed no hope of the situation ever getting better. Somehow these words seemed to soothe his own frantic worries – and seemed also to calm his guests into a willing submission to his optimistic plans!

But these words truly are words of hope that if it is not alright now, then it's because it is not the end – there is more to come and that more will be worth the wait. Spoken earnestly by this idealistic passionate young Indian man in different scenarios throughout the film, they were words which invited trust in moments when there seemed to be little visible evidence to warrant that trust. These words invited the guests to wait patiently and in hope that there would be resolution and change. Their barely built hotel and the chaos of the rooms would one day become home, would one day become the place they retreated to for refuge and comfort and love. But they would need to wait – in hope. The one woman who did not wait patiently but pushed against the circumstances, damaging her spirit in the process, left prematurely and never did experience the rewards that the others enjoyed as their dilapidated hotel really was transformed into the place they called home.

Since then, I've found myself repeating that one line often in different situations where there seems to be no way out, and especially the final words, 'it's not the end'. If it's not alright, it's because it's not the end; but there will be an ending. Guaranteed. We just need to wait. And we need to be prepared that the fruit of our waiting may not be what we expected; in fact, it rarely is, which is why we need to reassure our hearts that we are waiting for a person to act rather than for a problem to be resolved. And the person we are waiting for is the wisest, kindest, most compassionate, loving, understanding presence in our lives who will act on our behalf in keeping with the depths of his love for us and the depths of his purposes – not just for our lives – but for all the ways in which our lives are part of a purpose-held world. So, we wait for hope to appear, for hope to reappear.

And it is a clear word of hope that God gives to Habakkuk in 2:3. We don't know how long he had waited in that watchtower for God, but his wait was rewarded. God shares with him a vision of the future, a vision whose fulfilment would demand patience. The Contemporary English Version of this verse is helpfully clear here, 'At the time I have decided, my words will come true. You can trust what I say about the future. It may take a long time, *but keep on waiting* – it will happen!' With a single sentence, we are confronted with the reality that God's timing is not our timing. Wrapped within the hope-filled waiting for God's full answer to our 'How long?' questions and to our 'Why?' and 'How?' questions is an invitation to look beyond the immediate circumstances and what they seem to be telling us about God and life and how things should be working – and to believe that the God who has bound himself to us with the cords of loving kindness and compassion is at work.

When Habakkuk entered his watchtower, it seems that he had let go of so much and now his hands were empty enough of his own plans and purposes to receive the revelation of God's purposes. There was nothing he could do to change the upheaval that was about to take place in his beloved Judah; he could only settle down in trust that the God he had always known would vindicate his name and bring about redemption for his people. His trust would be well rewarded. God would indeed redeem his people. He would purify and draw them back to himself at great cost – but that was all for a future time. Right now, Habakkuk was being asked to trust God in this very moment of his own personal history. He was being asked to live out of a trust in the God of ruined places and dreams and hopes, and to believe that, one day, this God would reveal the full wonder of his glory, not just within the boundaried contours of Israel, but throughout the world; that, one day, the earth would be filled with the knowledge of the glory of God. One day, not only would the ruined city of Jerusalem be rebuilt and the ruined lives of its captive people restored, but the earth itself would be transformed through the redemption that was to come. Habakkuk was shown a vision for the future and was asked to trust the God who held that future.

We are asked nothing less than this in the harder moments of our own histories: to trust that God is working out his purposes for our lives and the lives of those we care about. He does so in ways and within a timeframe that we can barely comprehend, but which one day will be clear not only to us, but to those who have witnessed our journey, who have walked with us through our ruins, and who will one day bear testimony to the steadfast love of the Lord displayed in our own lives. We are asked to trust and to live out of that trust in humble dependence on God, in quiet surrender to his wisdom, in confident surrender to his love. As we do so, we may find that our 'Why?' and 'How?' questions change, that they are merely stepping stones to a bigger question: 'What transformation is God desiring here and what is my part in it?'

God invites us to believe and trust that although the healing of our wounds, the untying of the knotted threads of our circumstances, the work of grief and forgiveness, of relinquishing and hope-building, may take longer than we'd want it to, it will happen. It will happen in God's own time. And it will not be overdue a single day.

In 2:3, God shares with Habakkuk a perspective on time that isn't governed by our need for closure and answers but by God's eternal purposes. God assures Habakkuk that there *is* an answer to the question 'How long?' and that answer is: 'Trust me; trust my timing even when it doesn't seem like anything good or purposeful is happening.' God is unwrapping his purposes for our lives, our world, according to his own wisdom. If we are ever to experience the presence of God among the ruins of our lives in transformative ways, then we will need to relinquish our control over the timing of God's working in our lives and our worlds; to relinquish the demand that God come through for us according to our understanding of what wise timing looks like.

I'm discovering that, as I acknowledge and surrender to God's control over the timing in my life, on my best days I am becoming more rested, less anxious, more willing to wait for God to act; to trust God to come to me with healing and hope for all that is yet to be. It is this trust that God seems to want to strengthen and affirm in Habakkuk's own life. It is a trust that will carry him on into hope and into a future he can barely imagine as he sits there in his tower. It is a trust God revels in.

Practices

I'd like to suggest two different practices which you might find helpful to engage with as you continue to reflect on this chapter. The first practice sets us up to listen to God's word.

Reading with our hearts

When Habakkuk climbed into his tower, he was intentionally looking for an undistracted place to be with God. In the silence of the tower, he listened, expectantly, for God's word. A well-established way of listening to God's word which dates back to the Middle Ages is the practice of sacred reading or *lectio divina* as it was known centuries ago. This is a way of reading which invites us to slow down, to pay attention to a short passage of scripture, to listen to that scripture with our hearts as well as our heads. So often we approach the Bible with a scalpel or a pick axe or a drill ready to take it apart, dissect and analyse, dig deep and plunder its treasures. This more inductive approach to studying the Bible is particularly helpful for enriching our knowledge, but we can sometimes get so lost in gathering information that we miss the transformation which the Holy Spirit longs to bring into our lives as he draws us into a heart-to-heart encounter with God.

So how do we engage with this transformative way of encountering God through scripture?

We begin, as Habakkuk did, by finding a quiet space where we can be as undistracted as possible (and that space might be the corner seat on the bus into work), and then, very intentionally, we acknowledge that we are in the presence of God. We might just want to very gently breathe a prayer such as, 'God you are here, speak to me now,' just to settle our minds and help us to focus.

We then begin to *read* out loud (or listen to) a few verses from the Bible. A passage from the Psalms or the Gospels might be a good place to start, but any passage of scripture works. At this time, we are not looking at a lengthy block of scripture, but a shorter passage to soak in. Read (or listen to) the passage a few times and, as you do, notice if there is a word or phrase which seems to grab your attention, which seems to pop up above all the other words or phrases.

When you've identified that word or phrase, pause for a few moments to *reflect* on why *this* word, *this* phrase? How does it connect with your life? Do you sense any invitation from God through this word or phrase? Does it comfort or confront you? Does it challenge or encourage you? Mull it over; allow whatever thoughts or feelings that are stirred to be there.

Then talk with God about your *response* to that word or phrase and how it has affected you.

Just recently I was reading Isaiah 43:1–4, a passage I'm very familiar with. That morning, the word 'honoured' (v. 4) seemed to jump out at me. It's not a word that I normally encounter in my days, but I sensed God was wanting me to know that in his eyes, I was honoured. God's invitation to me that morning was to turn my eyes away from those places where I felt inadequate and unworthy, and to see myself through his eyes, to believe him when he spoke those words to my heart. I am honoured. As I reflected more on this and as I shared my thoughts with the Lord, I sensed the Lord inviting me to think more creatively about what living as a God-honoured woman would look like through the rest of the day. That word was a very tender gift from God at a time when I was feeling undeserving of the Lord's attention, let alone his honouring. It became a transformative moment for me and one which I'm still working through.

Finally, take a few moments just to *rest* quietly in God's presence, knowing that as you step into the next thing to do, you continue to be in God's presence, known and held in his love.

The practice of stopping

Do you remember the Green Cross Code? Some of us grew up with it and remember it well. It came into being in 1970 when the UK government launched a new road safety campaign for children of primary school age. The code was very simple – 'Stop! Look! Listen!' These three simple words were taught and drilled and practised in order to protect and to keep children safe when they were out and about on the streets and the roads. They were intended to keep them alive in traffic.

At the beginning of chapter 2, Habakkuk seems to be engaging with a spiritual version of the Green Cross Code. He stops; he steps back from the traffic of his circumstances; he climbs up into the watchtower and there he looks for God's word; he waits and he listens for God to speak to him.

Habakkuk's actions here are such a good model for us when we are bruised or bewildered or buffeted by what is going on in our lives.

This stopping and withdrawing is not an attempt to escape from the reality of our situation, as much as it is a deliberate stepping away from it in order to gain a renewed perspective from God.

The intent of this time is to stop rushing ahead with our own agenda or fix-it mode. The intent is to put a stop to the default mode of 'business as usual' and to look intentionally at our lives, at what is happening in them. We look at the circumstances in which we find ourselves to discern what God is doing in them and through them. We look at the patterns of our lives for evidence of where God is present and working in those patterns. We listen for what God has to say to us in and through those circumstances. We listen to his word, we listen to godly men and women as they unwrap that word, as they share the life of that word in the counsel and encouragement they give us.

To put this into practice, pause for a moment to think if there is a situation, a relationship, a challenge or a question in your life right now which invites you into the wisdom of the Green Cross Code. As you think of the situation:

Stop
Is there anything which you may need to stop
    doing
    being
    feeling
    thinking
in order more intentionally to place yourself in a space where God can most easily reach you?

Look
What do you sense God may be wanting you to see, to discern in the situation about
    yourself?
    God?
    the circumstances and people involved?

Listen

As you sit quietly in the presence of God what do you sense God may be saying to you about the situation, and also about his involvement in it, his perspective on it, his purpose in it? Are there any scriptures which come to mind? A word from a song or a sermon? A word from a conversation which seems to be soaked in the wisdom and truth of God?

Bring all of your reflections together in a prayer which expresses your confidence in God's power and willingness to keep you safe in the traffic of the situations, the relationships, the challenges you have brought to him.

Chapter 5

Of plastic bottles, empty tin cans and trust

Look at that man, bloated by self-importance –
   full of himself but soul-empty.
But the person in right standing before God
   through loyal and steady believing
   is fully alive, *really* alive.

HABAKKUK 2:4 (*The Message*)

**The fundamental fact of existence is that this trust in God,
this faith, is the firm foundation under everything that
makes life worth living.**

HEBREWS 11:1 (*The Message*)

When the earthquake hit, I was fast asleep at home in Taichung,
Taiwan. It was 3.00 am on the morning of 21 September 1999 when
I woke to pitch black, the sound of crashing dishes and the listing
heaving of my bedroom floor and walls. Guided by the shouts and
screams in the courtyard five floors below, I made my way in the
darkness down the back stairs and on to the street where I stood
with my neighbours, shivering in the howling, shrieking wind that
I discovered accompanies an earthquake. As the foundations of the
earth moved, and the foundations of our building shook and shook,
we held on to each other for comfort, mute in our fear.

Thousands died that night. Many of those who lived in the taller
high-rise apartment buildings died because the support structures
of their buildings, which should have been filled with high grade
cement, were in fact filled with empty plastic bottles and tin

cooking oil containers. This criminal flimsiness had somehow been sufficient enough to withstand the many storms and typhoons which we experienced living on the island, but when this devastating earthquake hit, these internal fillers proved inadequate to withstand the impact, and the buildings came crashing down. For months after the earthquake, parts of the city continued to lie in ruins, uninhabitable, forsaken, rat-ridden and desolate. It took a long time for the city to recover, for the people who went through that experience to feel safe again.

Thankfully, not many of us will experience a literal earthquake but, for those who do, the experience can be life-changing, the aftershocks reverberating down through the years in different ways. Over a lifetime, though, few of us will escape events which both threaten and reveal the support structures of our lives with unambiguous clarity. It doesn't take a 921, as the Taiwan earthquake came to be known, or a 7/7 or 9/11, equally devastating earthquakes of human making, to shake the foundations of our lives, our security, our sense of safety, or our sense of being 'at home' in our world, and to leave us shivering in the ruins.

There are times when the earthquakes which arrive in our lives are of our own making; a result of our own sin, or unwise choices or decisions, and they can have devastating consequences. Most of the time, though, the earthquakes of our lives come unprovoked and without warning; they come at unexpected and inconvenient times (is there ever a convenient time for an earthquake?), and leave us stunned and shaken. Later, perhaps, we can measure their strength and the extent of their impact, but very rarely can we predict when they will arrive if there has been nothing to raise the alarm, if there has been no time to prepare for that moment. A call at midnight, a knock on the door in the early morning, the quiet pause before the consultant speaks, the text on the phone, the flashing glance of a speeding car – and in a heartbeat the trajectory of our lives is changed. In a life-shaping moment, our foundations are assaulted, and all we have trusted for support, for stability, is brought to the brink of collapse. The extent of the damage that occurs will be determined largely by the material with which we have built our foundations, our support beams.

Japan has become a world leader in building earthquake-proof structures, probably out of necessity as the whole island, criss-crossed with fault lines, is a massive earthquake zone. Japanese engineers have learned that in order to minimise the damage which an earthquake can cause, the foundations of the buildings must be designed with the utmost care, imagination and skill. Lives depend on the quality of those foundations.

Life can be an earthquake zone and we need to be even wiser than Japanese engineers in laying foundations which will be able to withstand shaking without collapsing. The building material of our foundations matters. The substance of our support structures does make a difference when the earthquakes of our lives hit hard.

In Psalm 11:3 David asks, 'When the foundations are destroyed, what can the righteous do?' (NIV). It's a genuine question and one which God addresses with Habakkuk in this chapter. The earthquake of God's revelation to Habakkuk has shaken so many questions out of him. Chapter 1 was full of them. Now here in chapter 2, God begins answering those questions with a foundation-laying truth that, in contrast to the proud who trust in themselves, 'the righteous live by their faith' (v. 4, NRSV). Hundreds of years later, the writer to the Hebrews asserts that, 'faith is the firm foundation under everything that makes life worth living' (Hebrews 11:1, *THE MESSAGE*). Spanning the centuries between the books of Habakkuk and Hebrews is this unshakeable truth: the most earthquake-proof foundation for our lives is a confident trust in God. In contrast to those who live independently of God, proudly trusting in the plastic bottles and empty tin cans of their own resources, those whom God has declared righteous are to live with him within an ongoing, faithful relationship of trust.

When Jenny was undergoing her multiple cancer treatments, there were moments when the foundations of trust that I had built over the years were battered by questions I hardly knew were there until they surfaced. They were questions which were focused primarily on the character of God:

- I asked why a God who was a healer did not heal Jenny.
- I asked why a God who was the sovereign Lord of all creation could not or would not create an army of non-cancerous cells to wipe out Jenny's cancer cells.
- I asked why a God who could control the movement of stars and storms could not or would not control the movement and spread of this awful malignancy.
- I asked why a God of love and tender compassion and mercy would allow such awfulness in the child of his love.

Given the circumstances, it's not unreasonable to assume that Habakkuk had his own trust questions too as he faced the reality of what God was planning to do:

- How could he trust in the holiness and righteousness of God when those very qualities seemed to be compromised by God's deliberate use of a corrupt and proud, violent, idol-worshipping nation?
- How could he trust in God's covenant commitment of love to his people if he was now planning on wiping them out at the hands of the Babylonians?
- How could he trust in God's justice when both he and God are agreed that the cruelty of the Babylonians was callous and well documented and well in excess of what Habakkuk believed was fair punishment for Judah's sins?

Throughout the rest of this chapter, God pours out truth upon truth, reinforcing the foundations of faith which had long been present in Habakkuk's life. He reveals the truth of his unchanging character, the truth of his unwavering purposes for his people and the truth of his constant presence with them. God unfolds this truth in the context of contrasts between the lives of those who actively trust in God and the lives of those whose own strength is their God (1:11), the proud, who trust only in themselves, and who as a consequence, are 'soul-empty' (2:4, *The Message*).

The truth of his character

In his confrontation with God over God's plans in chapter 1, Habakkuk had appealed to God's holiness, his covenant love, his faithfulness and justice. And now it seems God was asking Habakkuk to trust that he had not changed; he was still the same God that Habakkuk had always believed him to be and had always trusted him to be. God had not changed, but the perspective from which Habakkuk was viewing him had changed – and, as a result, his understanding of God now needed to change.

Sometime after Jenny died, one of my students, Jules, gently asked, 'Mags, do you still believe in the goodness of God?' It was a quiet moment in a far-reaching conversation about God's character, and an insightful question. Of all God's characteristics, the goodness of God has been recognised as foundational to all his other attributes. When our belief and trust in the goodness of God breaks down, the foundations really are under attack. The goodness of God had always been the one attribute of God which I believed I had a steady hold on. In fact, Jeremiah 32:40–41 (NIV) have been the anchor verses of my life for over 30 years; 'I will make an everlasting covenant with them: I will never stop doing good to them… I will rejoice in doing them good.' Over the years, God had taught me to frame my life with his goodness; to trust that the circumstances of my life, whatever their dimensions, were actually held within the frame of his goodness. I had learned through some tough experiences not to judge God's goodness by my circumstances, but to judge and evaluate my circumstances within the framework of God's goodness. But the journey I'd travelled through Jenny's suffering had brought me to new depths of understanding and experiencing – and also at times questioning – the nature of his goodness. But on that quiet evening, I didn't need to think too much before answering Jules that more than ever I believed in *the mystery* of God's goodness. Over those long months, I had come to understand as never before that there was a profound *mystery* to the goodness of God, and that resting in that mystery brought both peace and release.

This acceptance did nothing to change the circumstances, but I seemed to be changing in and through those circumstances as I surrendered daily to the truth of who I believed God to be, and to be for me. I realised that I was slowly becoming more free of dependence on external signs of God's goodness, and more willing to trust that his goodness was at work in ways I couldn't fathom. I was becoming less demanding that life work out according to my plans, on my schedule, according to my wisdom.

Looking back over these years, I am profoundly grateful for the ways that God has been moving me away from living so much on the choppy surface of my circumstances and into a new place of trusting dependence on him. But I am aware that there are depths yet to be discovered, and as welcome as this restful place is, the journey still beckons.

The truth of his purposes

Habakkuk had been deeply concerned with the ways in which God seemed to be compromising his holiness and his justice in his use of the Babylonians. In the largest portion of chapter 2, God reveals to Habakkuk that he could be trusted because, far from letting them get away with their cruelty and their corrupt lifestyles and practices, he was going to ensure that the Babylonians would get what they deserved for their barbarity (v. 6). They would drink from the cup of the Lord's judgement (v. 16) and they would be cut down (v. 17). God would work in accordance with his holiness and justice; Habakkuk would probably never see this happening as it would be another 70 years or so before this empire would fall, but it did happen. In 539BC, the Babylonian empire ceased to be the great world power it once was, as Babylon was captured by King Cyrus. God has such a long-term perspective on the unwrapping of his purposes, and it seems that, again, Habakkuk is confronted with an invitation to trust the long patience of God in his dealings with what was out of kilter, what was unjust in his world.

When we have been wronged, when we have been betrayed, misrepresented, misunderstood, mistreated in significant ways, the willingness to trust that God is working out his purposes for our greatest good, *even through* these circumstances, is never more needed and possibly never harder to do. Our natural desire is to set the record straight, to seek redress, to retaliate in some way. Peter reminds us that Jesus 'did not retaliate when he was insulted, nor threaten revenge when he suffered. He left his case in the hands of God, who always judges fairly' (1 Peter 2:23). This is what Habakkuk is being asked to trust here as God draws aside the curtain of time and reveals his long-term purposes to him.

In a scathing denunciation and judgement delivered through a series of five woes on Israel's enemy, who seem to be the epitome of those who live without any acknowledgement of God in their lives, God lays bare the utter inadequacy of trusting in the false gods, the plastic bottles and empty tin cans of security, power, status, wealth and pleasure which had so entranced the Babylonians. They would be left 'trembling and helpless' (v. 7), all their work done in vain (v. 13), their glory turned to shame (v. 16). Their end would be pitiful. God shares with his prophet the real-life consequences for those who live by trusting in themselves and their own resources to make life happen.

This revelation is both a comfort and a challenge. A comfort that God will not let wrongdoing go unpunished. No matter how long it takes, God's justice will not be compromised; he will act. But a challenge too, in our own lives to check if our foundations and the support structures of our lives are built with similar material – with what we have, what we do and who we are in the eyes of others.

It is so easy to distance ourselves from the Babylonians and their very obvious idolatry and proud, God–independent lives, but I wonder if there aren't some scary similarities, witnessed perhaps in our own desires to be seen to be doing well, financially, socially, spiritually. To be making a name for ourselves, to be known in circles that are important to us. I wonder too if we don't lie awake at night worrying about the future and how we can make it more secure, or if we don't gnaw on the old bone of a slight, or an offence, or a dismissive comment which leaves us mentally composing an email of shaming intent, or imagining a conversation in which we will let them have it. We may not be stockpiling other people's wealth, or building up an arsenal of weapons, or indulging in a wildly hedonistic lifestyle, or deliberately using others for our own advantage, but we might find that if we scrape away the crust of history and distance, there may be evidences of a similar drifting independence from God. If we lay our foundations with anything less than the truth of the character of God and our trust-filled commitment to that truth, then there is little to stand between us and the collapse of significant aspects of our lives when that earthquake hits.

Trust in the presence of God

The very last verse in chapter 2 is both an affirmation and a warning: 'But the Lord is in his holy temple. Let all the earth be silent before him.' The temple at Jerusalem was the space on earth where God declared he would be present with his people. 'This is my resting place forever… I will live here, for this is the home I desired' (Psalm 132:14). He had stated this through the psalmist– and here he is restating that truth. He is basically saying to Habakkuk, 'I am still here; I haven't gone anywhere and I'm not going anywhere. Quiet your words now; you are in the presence of the Holy One of Israel. No more words of protest or questioning now. It is enough.'

And, perhaps more than anything, it is this assurance of God's committed presence that we need as we sit like Job among the rubble of our lives, wondering how to rebuild. We need assurance that the God who holds all time in his hands, the God who holds all power in his hands, is the God who is present with us in all his rich fullness for the fullness of our need for him.

It was this assurance of the presence of God that Moses pleaded for when he was considering God's invitation to lead the children of Israel into the promised land. And God's response was, 'My Presence will go with you, and I will give you rest' (Exodus 33:14, NIV).

Over and over again, God assures his fearful, doubting, sinful children that he is with them. One of the very earliest promises that God gave to Abraham was 'Do not be afraid, for I am with you and will bless you' (Genesis 26:24). Through the prophet Isaiah, God said to his children, 'Don't be afraid, for I am with you. Don't be discouraged, for I am your God' (Isaiah 41:10). To his young prophet Jeremiah, God promised, 'I am with you to protect and rescue you' (Jeremiah 15:20). And then we have Jesus' own words to us as his disciples, 'I am with you always, even to the end of the age' (Matthew 28:20).

God's presence will bring rest to us too: quiet confidence and assurance in the face of all that is demanded of us in our earthquake days. The history of God's presence with his people, his care for them, his love and compassion, faithfulness and forgiveness, would form the basis of Habakkuk's hope for the future. A hope which he sang in a psalm of praise which began with terror and ended in triumph.

Practice: The prayer of attentiveness

One of the challenges for Habakkuk during this time of upheaval was to keep trusting God no matter what the circumstances were telling him; to trust that God was still committed to loving and guiding his people. Also, to resist the temptation to turn to his own resources, to make plans for his life that might have excluded God. Perhaps that is the challenge for us too when our worlds are shaking: to trust that God has not left the building and turned off the lights, but he is present in the darkness, in the confusion, in the storm; he is truly Emmanuel, God with us. But we don't need a trauma or a trouble to cause us to lose sight of God's love and faithfulness; we just need to live our days without an intentional engagement with God. And in the rush of our days this is so easy to do; to drift into a default mode of depending on our own resources, our own wisdom and before long, we discover that, in reality, we are living a God-independent life. Not a deliberate act of defiance, but a drifting away from active trust. But the danger in this drifting is the direction in which the drifting may take us. And for many of us, that direction is toward those places of self-sufficiency and self-reliance that God condemns in the Babylonians. One of the ways we can check this drifting is to become practiced in recognising and acknowledging God's presence with us throughout our days.

An ancient prayer practice which encourages us to be awake and aware of God's loving presence in our days is the 'Prayer of Examen'. It could also be called the prayer of attentiveness, as it invites us to be intentionally attentive to all the ways that God has been present in our days.

The prayer is a very simple one to practise; the heart of the prayer involves inviting the Lord to look back with us over our day through the lens of a couple of questions.

- Where have I experienced your presence in my day today? Experienced your love and kindness, your mercy and compassion, your strength and helpfulness?
- Where have you seemed hidden or absent?

I have practised this prayer almost daily for a number of years now and it has become part of the rhythm of my days, as habitual as brushing my teeth. At the end of my day, just before going up to bed,

I settle down on the sofa, quiet my heart and ask the Holy Spirit to lead me and to direct my thoughts as I review my day.

Then I recall the day, watching the events of that day cross my mind like the scenes of a film on a screen. I ask the Lord to press the pause button on any moment that he wants to draw my attention to, and especially to those places in my day where he was present. There are times when his presence is so obvious, and when I see those, I can thank him, but there are other times when I can miss him in the present moment, and I need the Holy Spirit to reveal to me where he was at that moment. Most times, those moments of presence are so ordinary that it would be easy to miss them: the help given by another customer as I tried to put air in my tyres, the email from a former student inviting me for dinner, the helpfulness of the bank employee when I phoned up to make a payment, an unexpected hour to myself because of a cancelled appointment. Such small moments in the grand scheme of things, but they are touches of God's faithful care, his goodness and love and compassion. Without this act of attentiveness, I can so easily miss them.

Sometimes I ask other questions: I may ask the Lord to help me see those times when I was most alive, most energised and engaged – and then those times when I felt the opposite; when I felt weary, unmotivated, energy-less. There may have been moments in my day when I became anxious or angry, fearful or insecure. As I pay attention to these different moments, I can invite the Lord to help me understand what was going on in me at those times. Helping to identify these different responses allows me to examine those areas of resistance and avoidance and the reasons for them, and to ask the Lord to transform me in those very places.

Then, to end the time, I ask the Lord to make me even more aware of his presence, his life and his love, tomorrow.

There have been times in my life when it's just not worked for this to be a daily practice. But I know how vital this is for my life, and so I've usually taken some time at the weekend where I can look back over the week that has just passed, and ask those same questions not of the day but of the week. I have friends who, as part of their rhythm of life with God, take a time once a month to pray this prayer. They may take an hour or more to do it, but the result is the same: the sense of an invitation from God to trust him more deliberately, and to be transformed more really.

Chapter 6

From the back door to the barn door – and beyond

For all those words which were written long ago are meant to teach us today; that when we read in the scriptures of the endurance of men and of all the help that God gave them in those days, we may be encouraged to go on hoping in our own time.

ROMANS 15:4 (J.B. Phillips)

I have heard all about you, Lord.
    I am filled with awe by your amazing works.
In this time of our deep need,
    help us again as you did in years gone by.
And in your anger, remember your mercy.

HABAKKUK 3:2

In some translations, Habakkuk 3:1 includes the word, 'shigionoth'. Although the meaning of 'shigionoth' is not too clear, it probably refers to the musical setting for the prayer, confirmed perhaps by the final instructions at the end of the chapter on how it should be sung. The Amplified Bible translates the heading as, 'A prayer of Habakkuk the prophet, set to wild, enthusiastic, *and* triumphal music.' This is no sweet lullaby to calm feverish fears; it is more of an anthem, accompanied by a full-throttled organ! It is a prayer of yearning for God's help at this time of deep need, a pleading for revival, a plea for mercy. It is a melody composed of notes drawn from the glorious redemption history of God's people and the strength of God's love for them. It is a song which on Habakkuk's lips flames as a beacon of hope, blazing into the bleakest of certain futures.

Various Bible dictionaries seem to be agreed that the most basic definition of hope is strong and *confident expectation*. When it's used in the scriptures, hope is invariably linked with God, with the unchanging character of God, and with the actions of God. Over and over again, the psalmists and the prophets encourage and exhort us to 'Hope in the Lord; for with the Lord there is unfailing love. His redemption overflows '(Psalm 130:7). We hope because 'he is our help and our shield' (Psalm 33:20), 'the fountain of living water' (Jeremiah 2:13) and 'our saviour' (Micah 7:7, NIV).

Hope may be an expectation, but it is not optimism, which seems to be a positive attitude that trusts things will get better just as soon as our circumstances change. Optimism is an encouraging quality to have when the clouds look grey and the picnic is due to start in an hour, but when it continues to ignore the reality of the truth of our situations it can be unhelpful, because it may hinder our turning to God. Hope, on the other hand, clings to a different reality; the solid reality of the love and involvement of God in our lives and the truth that he is present with us, for us, in us, in all that our days may be demanding of us. We don't place our hope in the expectation that the circumstances will change; we put our hope in God to be present in all the wonder of his person and purposes *in those very circumstances*. Biblical hope is not an escape from the reality of the situation we are in; it is rather a springboard into the courage to face our reality with the confidence that God is present and active and doing something which we may not understand now, but which one day will be fully revealed in all its wisdom.

Plaiting a rope of hope

My friend Karen gave me an insight into understanding what Habakkuk seems to be doing in these opening verses of chapter 3 when she told me of her experience of blizzards in her home state of North Dakota, which is situated on the Great Plains of North America. Karen was raised on a farm in that state, where vast stretches of land spread way off into the distance, a place where buffalo roam, solid against a clear horizon that seems to stretch forever. It is a landscape in which nothing blocks the fury of the snow blizzards, which in the winter months come driving in on savage winds, white-blanketing everything in sight. Karen told me of how the farmers in her area lived and worked through these blizzards and how they were able to continue to care for their livestock during them. She explained that when the farmers were given warning of the impending blizzard and the direction in which it was heading, they would gather their livestock into the barn and then they would tie a stout rope from the backdoor of the farmhouse to the barn door. When the blizzard hit with all its wild fury, and the animals needed feeding, or the cows needed milking, the farmer would walk the careful walk from the back door to the barn door, hand over hand along the rope. As he held on to the rope, there and back, he could move safely in a very dangerous and life-threatening situation. As long as he held on to that rope, no matter how bad the blizzard got, no matter how hungry the livestock got, everything would be fine. But she told me too that there were some who let go of the rope, who somehow lost their grip as the blizzard hit, and they died in the snow. Others had a rope, but for whatever reason, never used it. The result was the same; lost in the white expanse between the barn door and the backdoor, they never made it home through the swirling chaos and died within feet of their own back doors.

When we find ourselves in a blizzard of circumstances which blinds us to the presence of God and to any sign of his goodness, when we wake up to a whiteout of confusions, conflicts, fears and anxieties, it is easy to become disoriented, to lose our bearings, our balance, and to find ourselves whirling unsteadily in search of any familiar landmark with which to orient ourselves. It is for such a time that, like those North Dakotan farmers, we too need a rope to hang on to which will guide us home, which can lead us safely through the blizzard of our present circumstances and into safety. We need a rope of hope to hold on to just like the one which we witness Habakkuk plaiting in the early verses of this final chapter.

One of the key words for hope in the Old Testament is the word *tikvah*; it literally means 'cord' and is rooted in the Hebrew word *qavah* which means 'to bind together' or 'to stretch out'. There are just 33 mentions of the word 'hope' in the Old Testament, the majority of them appearing in the book of Job, which is a happy surprise. If we were to lay out the book of Job like a long table runner, the word 'hope' would appear as tiny gold knots in the dark fabric of Job's life, lighting up the darkness of the cloth.

What I find so poignant in considering this word is that, in the NIV, the first recorded use of the word hope in the Old Testament is found in Ruth 1:12. It appears in the context of a *loss* of hope. And there are lessons about hope to be found from this first appearance of the word. It is spoken by Naomi, a wounded elderly woman whose world, like Job's, had been devastated by multiple losses, and who has become embittered by those losses. The death of her husband and the death of her only sons took place in Moab, a land which wasn't her own and to which she had escaped with her husband when famine hit Israel. Famine was seen as an indicator of God's judgement, the land itself sharing in the consequences of the discipline of God. But Elimilech, whose name means 'my God is king', in his effort to escape from the place of God's discipline and judgement, took his family to Moab, a pagan nation who worshipped other gods, and where Yahweh was not recognised as king.

It was meant to be just a temporary move; a chance to survive until the famine in Israel was over. But the years passed and, as they did, the losses mounted, until there was nothing left for Naomi; no husband, no sons, no hope. So, with Ruth, her Moabite daughter-in-law, she headed home, back to Israel, bereft of everything that gave her life meaning, and bereft too of hope. When she arrived in Bethlehem, she was hardly recognisable as the woman who had left so many years previously. And she no longer owned the name her father had given her, 'Naomi', which means 'pleasant'. Now she chose a new name by which to define herself; she asked people to call her Mara, 'bitter'. Whatever hope she had was gone, stripped by the winds of bereavement and loneliness and the constant sense of being displaced among a foreign people and foreign gods. I wonder if this is what happens to us too when we lose our hold on hope. Do we become lost in our own bitterness, blind to goodness, blind to God, identified by words which are more descriptive of hopelessness than hope?

Reading through the pages of my journal, written during the harrowing months of Jenny's treatment and then later in those months after her death, certain words keep appearing. They seem to be a vocabulary list describing the reality of life in a ruined place. Over and over again I had written the words *lost*, *desolate*, *bewildered*, *disoriented*, *distressed*, *numb*, *overwhelmed*, *desperate*, *powerless*, *weary*, *self-focused*, *confused*, *angry*, *isolated* and *alone*. I've talked with others who have stood among their own ruins – and even though our experiences are different, we seem to share an intimate understanding of these words.

But in my journal, alongside the words which appeared in my lexicon of loss, I had also written out words of hope copied from the psalms; words such as those in Psalm 33:18 where the psalmist tells us that 'the Lord watches over those who fear him, those who *rely on his unfailing love*'. I wrote out David's words from Psalm 42:11, 'Why am I discouraged? Why is my heart so sad? I will put my *hope in God*! I will praise him again – my Savior and my God.' I exhorted myself to 'Hope in the Lord, for with the Lord there is unfailing love' (Psalm 130:7).

I soaked in these scriptures and my prayers were fuelled by their life-giving words, granting me permission and space to pour out the fullness of my heart to God, to omit nothing of the agony I felt in losing Jenny. But they also gave me words of praise, borrowed words to bring to God, words which acknowledged the wonder and grace of God's goodness and love as truth, even when I wasn't experiencing those qualities at that time – at least in ways that made sense to me.

Before rediscovering Habakkuk during that early morning wakeup call, I had spent hours reading and reflecting on Jeremiah's experiences expressed in the book of Lamentations, in which he records his journey through his own devastating grief over the destruction of Jerusalem. He writes, 'Peace has been stripped away, and I have forgotten what prosperity is. I cry out, "My splendour is gone! Everything I had hoped for from the LORD is lost!" The thought of my suffering and homelessness is bitter beyond words. I will never forget this awful time, as I grieve over my loss' (Lamentations 3:17–20). He is achingly honest about how he feels about the place he is currently inhabiting but, like Habakkuk, he didn't stay there. After chronicling the awfulness of his life during and after the Babylonian invasion, he continues, 'Yet I still dare to hope when I remember this: The faithful love of the LORD never ends! His mercies never cease. Great is his faithfulness; his mercies begin afresh each morning. I say to myself, 'The LORD is my inheritance; therefore, I will hope in him!'' (vv. 21–24).

Jeremiah intentionally turns his thoughts from the awfulness of his circumstances and calls to mind the character of God. He calls to mind God's great love and his unfailing compassion. And hope is born – not out of some willed act of stoic resolution, but as the fruit of a mind and heart that has been soaked in the truth of the character of God revealed in his word. While acknowledging the awful reality of the situation he is in, he is able to acknowledge too the weightier reality of God's unfailing covenant-committed love toward his people. The challenge he faced was of accepting the facts of the situation and the awfulness of those facts, and *at the same time*, embracing the truth of God's character, the strength of his love and faithfulness to his word – despite what the circumstances seemed to be saying. We sometimes make it an 'either/or' choice, feeling that one cancels out the other and that therefore we need to pick a side. Hope, however, reaches out both arms, embraces both sides, both truths, and holds them close. Hope acknowledges the reality that there can be no turning back, no going back to what has been true in the past. But there can be a going on, incorporating the past into a future that has yet to be shaped, but is capable of being shaped differently. This is hope.

Memories have been described as the seedbed of hope. As Jeremiah called to mind God's involvement in his own life, he shorthands for us what Habakkuk unpacks in this prayer, which is a robust testimony to the acts of God in the history of the children of Israel. Habakkuk doesn't just drop a bucket into the well of his own experience of God, but into the deeper well of the history of Israel's experience of God. As Habakkuk seems to watch these acts on the screen of his memory, as he recounts and records God's acts on behalf of his children, hope seems to stir in him. These irrefutable events, drawn from the history of God's involvement with his people, are incontestable evidence of God's commitment to his people which would continue despite the dreadfulness that was yet to come. They were objective facts from the history books of the people of Israel. God had acted in real time, and real space with real people and in real circumstances. Therefore, hope was possible.

So, Habakkuk plaits his rope of hope, thread over thread, event over event. Acts of redemption and rescuing and restoration even in the most horrific of circumstances are twined around with the strong threads of God's unchanging character: his covenant love and faithfulness, his power and his sovereignty over all creation. And as Habakkuk plaits his rope, prayer and worship and supplication rise from his heart, framed with awe and humility and longing that God be seen for who he truly is and that he works in the life of his people in judgement – but also in mercy and in power. The God of Israel's past was the God who would recreate her future. And it is in this truth that Habakkuk anchors his hope. He pleads with God, 'Help us again as you did in years gone by' (3:2) and then over and under, under and over, he plaits his rope of hope from all that God had done for his people in those 'years gone by'.

In years gone by

Specifically, he is reminded of how God redeemed Israel out of their slavery in Egypt and brought them into the promised land of Canaan. He chooses the most extravagant words to describe God and what he did during those days and then piles them on, word upon word. God's splendour is 'brilliant' (v. 3), his power is 'awesome' (v. 4). Heaven and earth, the totality of all that is, are filled with his glory and praise (v. 3). This is a God who 'shatters the everlasting mountains', who 'levels the eternal hills' (v. 6). This is a God who can take well-established, seemingly immovable obstacles and toss them aside in order to accomplish his purposes. This is a God unfazed by what has always been, what is established or entrenched, a God who is able to clear the ground for something completely new. He leaves the enemies of his people 'in distress' and 'trembling in terror' (v. 7). The God who rises out of these verses is an incontestably awesome God who is more than able to handle whatever it is that his people need from him. And amazingly, this is *our* God too; this is the same power of God for the needs of our lives too. How many of us, I wonder, sing the words to songs like 'How great is our God' or 'Our God is an awesome God' and yet, in the depths of our hearts, can't quite believe that this God would use that power on our behalf, would wade into the rubble of our lives and actually *do* something for us, something unexpected, something truly redemptive. That he would rescue us, bring us into a spacious place, and fight for us, for our dignity and our honour and our good. Would he, could he do this for us? And the answer is a resounding 'Yes'. We are his. We are the children of his love, the joy of his heart. Yes, he can. And so we can hope.

Habakkuk then reminds himself of all the times when God did something with large bodies of water – the Nile, the Jordan in flood, the parting of the Red Sea. The children of Israel were very fearful of large bodies of water, so in recounting how God rescued Israel through water, Habakkuk is reminding himself of all the times when Israel was in terrifying circumstances and God did not miraculously take them *out* of those circumstances, but *through* them, which is perhaps a greater miracle. In choosing to focus on these fear-filled incidents, Habakkuk is reminding himself – and us – that God is present in the most frightening circumstances of our lives. He is present when our fears rise like floodwaters and threaten to drown everything we have believed in or hoped for or counted on. God is present in all his power and love and compassion. God is with us. Later, the prophet Isaiah would write in Isaiah 43:2, 'When you go through deep waters, I will be with you.' Water in its natural state is unpredictable, and there are circumstances in our lives which are totally unpredictable and unstable and overwhelming – and as we read Habakkuk, we are reminded that these very circumstances were the means by which God redeemed his people. He had been their redeemer and saviour in the most awful of circumstances. And he would be that again for them. Those very circumstances would form the substance of a new reality.

He reminds himself too that God is able to suspend natural laws if he chooses to use this way to come to the aid of his people in their distress (v. 11). He is a champion, defending and defeating all who threaten to destroy his people, no matter how strong or capable, no matter how rapacious and powerful. God was able to rescue and to save, to redeem out of chaos, a people for his own glory (vv. 12–15). They are his, his own dearly loved children. He could no more abandon them than a nursing mother could forget the baby at her breast, as Isaiah so graphically put it (Isaiah 49:15).

Turn, turn, turn

As he plaits his rope of hope through these verses, we see Habakkuk turning away from his questions, his confusion and bewilderment, and turning toward the God of his hope. Because of the unchanging character of God and his love for his people, his purposes for their ultimate good, and his might and power in being able to deliver on his promises, to fulfil his purposes, there would be new life birthed from the pain which was coming. Each memory that Habakkuk plumbed turned him toward light, toward hope, toward life. Each turning was a sunflower moment turning him toward the face of God.

I really like sunflowers; they are an image of relentless hopefulness. Whenever the clouds seem to block out the sun, the sunflower turns its open, uplifted head towards the east, toward life and light. At her funeral, Jenny's closest friends brought large beautiful sunflowers to lay on her willow-woven casket. They were such a vivid representation of Jenny's life, especially in the darker days when we saw her turn so very deliberately towards joy and to life and to love. Those sunflowers on her casket were also a sign of hope for all of us who were at the funeral; that life would go on, somehow. That tears would one day cease for a while, that the pain which would never truly be erased would be eased, that the small events of which a life is composed would begin to matter again, and the hope of a new, different kind of living, would appear – one day.

However long or short our personal history with God may be, we can do something Habakkuk could never do; we can reach back to the testimony of the cross of Jesus and his resurrection and ascension. We can affirm with the writer to the Hebrews that our hope is anchored beyond the veil – beyond death, beyond life. Our hope is tied and knotted and secured to the life and death of Jesus and the love of God for us expressed in that life and death. Our hope is held within the outstretched arms of Jesus on the cross. And that will never change. Before his ascension, Jesus told his followers one last thing before he left them: 'I am with you always' (Matthew 28:20). Jesus had shared their lives, and now he was promising them – and us – that he would continue to be present, that he would continue to share their lives – our lives – until the moment when all of life, all of time, comes to an end. The truth of the cross, the resurrection and the ascension promise of the presence of Jesus is our strongest, most enduring hope of a new way of living; of a transformed future, rising up from the ruins of the old.

Practice: Mapping your spiritual journey

Habakkuk's rehearsal of the landmark events in Israel's national life and of God's involvement in those events built his hope that the God of the past was the God of the present and of the future. His deliberate recalling of those landmarks created an expectation of what might yet be possible in the future along with the reassurance that the God of his history would be the God who would be present with him in all that was yet to happen.

The practice of reflecting on our personal history with God – or mapping our spiritual journey, which is another term for this – can become a helpful means of identifying the important events in our journey with God and understanding how they have shaped our lives as we look back from the vantage point of time and distance and experience. It's not the events themselves that are as important to dwell on as the way in which those events have shaped us and our understanding of God. Therefore, the focus of this practice is on clearly discerning how God has been actively involved in our lives through different experiences, relationships, challenges, obstacles, gifts and blessings. It is a way of standing back and gaining perspective for the long haul of faith, helping us to build layers of hope out of the history of God's dealings in our lives. As we do this, we may be able to recognise his goodness and his faithfulness to us in the sweeping history of our lives. And this recognition can lead us into a greater trust and confidence, a greater freedom in worship, a greater hope for the present and the future.

These landmarks come in a variety of shapes and sizes: they can be relationships, events, locations, conversations, a conference, a book, a talk, circumstances, answers to prayer or no answers at all, and often many of those things all at the same time. The significance of the landmark doesn't depend on the nature or the size of the landmark itself, however, but on the impact that it has had on the landscape of our own lives, and the legacy of hope it leaves behind.

So how do we do it, and where do we begin?

There are a number of ways to engage in this practice of mapping our journey with God. I'd like to suggest two; one which involves words and one which involves images. For many of us, our interpretation of life is best done through images and their significance in our lives; for others, only words will do. Choose whichever one is best for you – but you might want to try the other too.

Using words

Preparation
Sit quietly for a few moments and allow your mind to wander over your life and the experiences that you have had of God. Don't filter anything; just allow your mind to drift over the landmark events of your life, over places of difficulty, of hurts or disappointments, of interactions with people, of turning points and transitions. Now, pause for a moment with an experience which you sense has shaped you significantly in some way. In what ways has that experience shaped you? How has it moved you in a certain direction in your understanding of God, or of yourself, of his purposes in your life and or in the world.

Mapping your journey
That one experience is part of a pattern of experiences which makes up the fabric of our lives. It is one thread in the plaiting of our own *tikvah*. As we map our journey, we will add more threads to our *tikvah* which will become stronger and stronger as we do so.

God uses many different encounters and experiences to reveal himself to us and to shape our lives, so reflect more deliberately on the following questions:

- Who are the key people who have shaped my life, and how did they do that?
  - What did I learn about God from them – if anything? (This might be positive or negative.)

- What are the key circumstances that have shaped me? In what ways have they shaped me?
    - How did God reveal himself through those circumstances? What images of God did those circumstances shape for me?

- What are the key choices, decisions and responses which have made a real difference in my life and how I live it? How did they do that?
    - How did God show up in those areas?

Using images

In this practice, you are going to create a mental picture album, a gallery of people or events or circumstances that have played a significant role in your life and that have shaped your relationship with God and your growth in knowing and becoming more like Jesus.

Allow your mind to wander over your life, without censoring anything, until it lands on an image of a person or a situation or a place which holds some significance for you. Place that mental photo in your photo album or on the wall of your picture gallery. Pause before your picture and ask yourself *why* this person or event? What significance did this particular photo have on your life or on your understanding of God at the time that the 'photo' was taken? What has been the legacy of this photo in your life? In what ways has it shaped your life?

Repeat this exercise until you feel that you have no more significant photos to place in your album at this time. Now if possible, glance through the entire album, stand back and look at the entire wall. What impression do you get of God's involvement in your life in bringing you to the place in which you stand today?

A combination

A way to combine words and images is to draw a couple of lines which represent the contours of your journey with God so far; they won't be parallel lines like a railway track, but more the image of a meandering river. Divide your river into ten-year segments; perhaps a bend in the river could indicate the movement into another ten-year segment. On one side of the river bank, place the people or places which were significant in your life during that ten-year period; on the other side, the events, circumstances, turning points or transitions which were significant. Do this for the whole of your life. As you look at the whole sweep of the river's course, what impression do you get of how your life has been shaped, and how God has been involved in your life through the years?

Attentiveness
A vital practice in helping us to grow in identifying those potentially transforming moments in our lives is the practice of attentiveness. We can learn to be more attentive to God and to how God is present in our days, attentive to ourselves, to our responses and reactions to events, to our dreams and desires and doubts and disappointments in the ordinary moments of our lives. We do this as we become increasingly aware that there are some experiences and/ or relationships which are particularly significant to us; they move us forward, stop us in our tracks, undo chains and free us from the past; they become for us not just landmarks but springboards into new and richer encounters with God and with life. There are questions we can ask ourselves which will enable us to grow in our attentiveness. For example, we can ask the following:

- Where was God in this experience, this conversation, this encounter?
- What do I sense God is wanting to say to me through this?
- Who is God inviting me to be, what is God inviting me to do through this?

As we grow in developing attentiveness in this way, we become increasingly aware that the God in whose presence we live constantly is with us, in that place, and he is not silent.

Chapter 7

What's in a name?

Even though the fig trees have no blossoms,
    and there are no grapes on the vines;
even though the olive crop fails,
    and the fields lie empty and barren;
even though the flocks die in the fields,
    and the cattle barns are empty,
yet I will rejoice in the Lord!
    I will be joyful in the God of my salvation!
The Sovereign Lord is my strength!
    He makes me as surefooted as a deer,
    able to tread upon the heights.

HABAKKUK 3:17–19

Circumstances may appear to wreck our lives and God's
plans, but God is not helpless among the ruins. Our broken
lives are not lost or useless. God's love is still working. He
comes in and takes the calamity and uses it victoriously,
working out His wonderful plan of love.

Eric Liddell[16]

Perhaps one of the hardest things to believe as we stand in the rubble
of our personal ruins is that there will be life after this devastating
loss, this breakdown, this betrayal, this deepest wounding, this sin.
To believe that there will ever be a meaningful future, that there
will ever be anything to look forward to again, can be so hard. We
can look at the reality of our circumstances now and believe that
the future will just be more of the same: the pain of the present
stretching way into the future with no respite or reprieve. It can be so
hard to imagine a redemptive outcome, to believe that despite these

circumstances there will be new life; that there will be a new dawn; and that this new dawn will bring new possibilities for change and transformation. To believe that although weeping may endure for a night, joy *does* come in the morning; and morning always comes.

There may be times when we look at our lives and inwardly whisper, 'If these circumstances were different, then life might have a chance to flourish, I might live again.' And yet Eric Liddell, who died as a missionary in a Japanese prisoner-of-war camp, affirmed the truth that although 'circumstances may appear to wreck our lives and God's plans, God is not helpless among the ruins'. Thousands of years earlier, Habakkuk affirmed, 'Even *though* these circumstances are as bad as they can get and they are not going to change any time soon, *yet* I will not only live, but I will live fully, with a depth of joy and a commitment to life which will take me beyond these circumstances and into a redemptive, hopeful place.'

Habakkuk isn't playing peek-a-boo with reality here; he is facing it fully. Just before this jubilant declaration, he tells us that he trembled inside, his lips quivered in fear, his legs gave way and he shook in terror (3:16). It is a comprehensive description of the emotional and physical effects of fear. He knows what is coming and he is very, very afraid. But then he seems to take in the deepest of breaths and breathes out this awesome song of confident exultation and hope which is spring-boarded from the word 'yet'.

'Yet' is a pivotal word; it is a choice word. Habakkuk *chooses* to focus on the unchanging character of God rather than on his circumstances and what they may or may not be telling him about God, because nothing in his circumstances has changed, or will change any time soon. There is systemic corruption: the people continue to be depraved; God has not changed his mind with regards to his judgement of Judah; the land is still destined to be invaded. The destruction and devastation and deprivation which Habakkuk depicts in the layering of his 'even though's in verse 17 are an inevitable consequence of the direction in which Judah has been moving.

But Habakkuk has changed. He had clearly heard God's word; he had entrusted himself to that word; he has roped himself to the God of hope; and as a result he is transformed from the desperate and distressed prophet we meet in the opening words of the book, to this confident, exultant, exuberant man of hopefulness. On the lips of Habakkuk, this word 'Yet' is a word of deepest confidence that grabs the reality of the circumstances by the throat and declares:

> No, this is not where it ends! This is not the end of God's story. My God is the God of a love that does not let go, who has a dream for my life that does not die, a purpose for my life that cannot, will not be abandoned *even* among these ruins. This is the God whose very being has become my joy, my crazy dancing-in-the-ruins joy. And I will dance. I will run across the mountain tops. I will rejoice. I will.[17]

He rejects what could be a natural despair for a joy that has nothing to do with his circumstances and everything to do with the person of the God who is present *in* those very circumstances, and who promises that there is life beyond all of this loss, all of this death. Joan Chittister writes,

> Despair cements us in the present. Hope sends us dancing around dark corners trusting in a tomorrow we cannot see because of the multiple pasts of life which we cannot forget. Despair says there is no place to go but here.[18]

And it is a lie; a lie which Habakkuk rejects as he anchors himself in the truth of who God is, expressed through the different names for God that our Bibles reveal in the original languages in which they were written.

On the night before Jenny's funeral, I asked God a question that all of us at some stage or other will end up asking, as we sit like Job among the rubble of what's left of our dreams, our hopes, our longings, our life. When we come face to face with a God who we may feel has profoundly disappointed us, who seems to have let us down, who seems to have abandoned us, we may ask, 'Who are you? Really, who are you?' The name which God gave me for himself that evening was 'Emmanuel', God with us, present with us in all of our pain, all of our grief, all of our hopelessness. It was the name which pulsed into my waking moments just a year after Jenny's death: 'Even though… even here… Emmanuel'. But God has many other names as well, and Habakkuk evokes three of them here.

Yahweh

He will 'rejoice in the LORD' (3:18), in *Yahweh*, the name by which God first made himself known to Moses when he revealed that name in the context of his care for his suffering people: 'God *heard* their groaning and he *remembered* his covenant with Abraham, with Isaac and with Jacob. So God *looked on* the Israelites and *was concerned* about them' (Exodus 2:24, NIV). Then he states, 'I have come down to *rescue* them' (Exodus 3:8). And he promises Moses, '*I will be with you*' (Exodus 3:12). The italicised verbs speak of a God who is acutely aware of his people's needs, who is engaged and involved. A stunned Moses had no idea of the name of the one he was speaking with. What is the name of this God? Like so many of us, he asks, 'Who are you?' And it is then that God reveals his personal name for the first time, telling Moses that he is 'Yahweh, the God of your ancestors – the God of Abraham, the God of Isaac and the God of Jacob… This is my eternal name, my name to remember for all generations' (Exodus 3:15). Yahweh is the God who is present, who is compassionate, who is profoundly concerned for his people. In referring to himself as *Yahweh*, God is saying to Moses – and to us too – 'I am here with you, right now, right here, with love and care and concern for all that you are and all that you are facing in your life. Wherever you are, that's where I am too. This is my promise to you.'

It looked for a while as though Habakkuk had grounds for believing that Yahweh had ceased to be present, that he had ceased to care, that he was reneging on his covenant with his people, but through his honest engagement with God, Habakkuk was released to rejoice in the God he'd always known – the God who is *Yahweh*. He could rejoice in Yahweh because it meant that whatever happened next, he was not alone. Judah was not alone. Yahweh, the ever-present God, was going to be with them through it all. And it would be enough.

And perhaps this is what we need to know when we are standing in our own ruins – that we don't stand alone. Whatever the circumstances may be telling us, God *is* with us. God *is* present with us. Always. But there can be times when we are not aware of his presence, when we are blind to the strength of his committed love for us.

In Romans 8:38–39, the apostle Paul builds his case for the indefatigable love of God for us in an outpouring of words which culminates in the statement that 'nothing in all creation will ever be able to separate us from the love of God that is revealed in Christ Jesus our Lord'. It is a breathtaking truth – *nothing* can ever separate us from his love – but the reality is that there are many things which can separate us from the *experience* of that love.

There may be sin and the accompanying awful weight of guilt and shame and regret. There may be wounds from the past that have not been healed and we are nursing the fears, the anger, the oozing grudges, the hurts and the resentments caused by those wounds. There may be worries for the future which grab our hearts in the middle of a sleepless night, which suck the air out of the words, 'Jesus loves me this I know' and which leave us gasping in fear for all that might happen, and about which we feel helpless and out of control – especially at three o'clock in the morning. And there are places in the present which question belief in a loving God: unmet expectations, unrealised dreams, unanswered prayers; all of these can conspire to rob us of our trust, our hope in the love of God. Where do we go from here? How do we bridge the gap between the truth of God's word and the sometime reality of our lived experience of God in our world?

We do a Habakkuk!

We don't look around in the rubble for the exit sign; we look back again at the character of God revealed for us in his word. We soak our souls in the truth that our God is the heart-achingly hopeful Father who waits for us to come home and who, at the slightest hint on the wind of our pig-penned self, comes running toward us with open arms, ignoring our protestations of unworthiness to be so loved, so very welcoming. We soak in the truth of a God who looks at us in the lostness of our elder-brother righteousness, and gently reminds us that 'all I have is yours'. We may have never asked for what he was waiting, longing, to give us, so we live upright but uptight, joy-deprived, sparse lives. We read the stories of the great ones like David, Moses, Peter and Paul and see in them the God who doesn't give up on us but who pursues us with passion and with purpose. And this is the same God whom the apostle John tells us came and lived among us, right where we are, as we are (John 1:14). The incarnate covenant love of God held babies, held sorrow, noticed the dying of sparrows and the grieving of a son-lost widow, healed the crippling wounds of sin and the wounded bodies and minds crippled by disease and demons. This Love is a love that weeps at the death of his friend Lazarus, weeps with salvation-longing over Jerusalem, weeps too for himself in the Garden of Gethsemane as he anticipates the dreadful loneliness of his own death. It is a love that weeps for us, with us, now and wherever we may be in the days to come.

This is our Yahweh; the living presence of God among his people. He is the God who never leaves us to stand on our own in the ruins of our lives, but who comes and stands with us in them. And who reassures us that because his name is also *Elohim* – we can look forward to a different future from the one which we are experiencing now.

Elohim

Habakkuk announces that he will joy in *Elohim*, the God of his salvation (3:18), the God who is the mighty creator of all things. Elohim is the first title of God we encounter in the very first verse of the Bible: 'In the beginning *God* created…'. Elohim is the strong, powerful God who not only creates and sustains the world, but creates and sustains the life of every creature in that world. He is the God who speaks galaxies and glow worms into being! 'Then God said…' is repeated over and over again in the opening chapter of our Bibles. In the Old Testament, *Elohim* is used most often when the writer is emphasising God's might and creative power.

In choosing to rejoice in Elohim, Habakkuk was embracing the possibility of new beginnings, of re-creation, of redemption for his people. His exultant declaration reassures his heart that the one who created the heavens and the earth and all that was out of nothing, is able to create something new and fresh and healthy out of the swampy mess that he and his people were in at that time. Habakkuk is rejoicing because he believes that God is capable of restoring and redeeming all that is deformed and distorted and in need of renewing in the lives of his children. He is rejoicing because Elohim is also the name which the scriptures use when describing the covenant-keeping God of the Old Testament.

The first time we see Elohim making a covenant with anyone, it is with Noah. And the covenant he made was wrapped in his promise not to destroy the earth again with water (Genesis 9:11). But more, God placed a rainbow in the skies as a sign of his covenant with all the creatures of the earth (Genesis 9:17). Habakkuk knew that the God who placed rainbows in the skies was the God who would keep his other covenant promises to his people, to be their God forever. As long as there was a God who kept his promises, Habakkuk knew that his people would not be wiped out, however bad the circumstances were. And as long as there were rainbows in the sky, Habakkuk knew that God would not forget his people and he would not forget his solemn covenant with them.

And it is no less true for us as we recognise the truth that we live within the care of a God who is both the creator and the re-creator of our lives. In Ephesians 2:10 Paul reminds us that we are God's creation, we are his workmanship, his masterpiece, created anew in Christ Jesus. The opening words of John's Gospel introduce us to the Word, who was 'with God' and 'was God' and who 'existed in the beginning with God' and who 'gave life to everything that was created' (John 1:1–4). The God of our salvation has a name: it is Jesus, our Saviour. He is Life itself, and he can breathe new life into us in the very places where we are dying; he can raise life out of the deepest graves where we have laid our dreams and hopes. He is Christ, the Lord of Life, Lord over death. This is our God, this is our *Lord*.

Yahweh Adonai

And this is the final name in which Habakkuk will rest his weary soul. *Yahweh Adonai*, the Sovereign LORD, is his strength. This name signifies sovereign power, supreme authority and complete ownership. But the wonder of this power, this authority and strength is that it is exercised on behalf of those who have come under his care and protection. The word 'Adonai' means master or lord. In the Old Testament, the relationship between master and servant was a dim reflection of the relationship between Adonai and his children, but a reflection nonetheless. That relationship was not tyrannical, but often a relationship of love and loyalty in which the servant was assured that his lord, his master, had all the resources necessary to provide for him. Everything that was needed for the servant to live and to fulfil his duties was provided for. The servant never needed to worry about his food or shelter, his clothing or any other necessities – those things were the responsibility of the master to provide. His only responsibility was to be faithful and available and obedient. It was a relationship of mutual accessibility.

In choosing to declare that Yahweh Adonai – the Sovereign Lord – is his strength, Habakkuk is placing himself firmly under the care, the shelter, the provision and the protection of the one who would exercise his sovereign wisdom and kindness and power on his behalf – whatever the future.

And he has come full circle. At the end of this journey, he has arrived at the place from which he began when he declared that his God is the Lord, the Holy One, the eternal, the Rock. It's been a journey which has brought him all the way back home to the truths that he had always known and believed, only to own them again, with greater depth of insight and trust. And I wonder if that isn't where our own journey with God through the landscape of our own ruins doesn't eventually end up? Not so much with new truth, perhaps, as much as with new depth and conviction and commitment to old truths which we've always believed about God.

Last year, I was corresponding with a friend who was going through some significant and pain-filled losses in her life and, during the course of our correspondence, I shared with her something of what I had learned from my experience of losing Jenny, and I realised that like Habakkuk, I too had come full circle. In that email, sent almost four years after Jenny's death, I wrote,

> The surrender is ongoing, as you can imagine. But I have to say that my experience with the Lord through Jenny's cancer and death has had a massive impact on my theology and how I am now viewing the Lord. He has become so much more than I ever expected. More merciful, more generous, more real and accepting. Less judgemental, less narrow, less demanding somehow. Not sure how to explain it except to say that something very fundamental has changed in my relationship with the Lord and I so hope it doesn't change back!

In the car that evening before Jenny's funeral, I had said to the Lord, 'You need to be more.' His reply was 'More I can do – but you need to trust me.' As I was writing my email, it came as the gentlest of realisations that I had actually come to know the Lord as 'more' in ways I could never have imagined when the journey with Jenny's cancer began. Above all, I have experienced him as more of the wise, tender, compassionate, strong Father whose heart Jesus portrayed for us so clearly in his own life as we watch him walking through the pages of the Gospels: 'Anyone who has seen me has seen the Father' (John 14:9).

Knowing the names of God as Habakkuk did is not a theological coup! In the abstract, this knowledge is just information, not transformation. Habakkuk's understanding of the truths encapsulated in the names of God moves him to this final assertion of purpose and intent and fearless action; a tremendous testimony of transformation: 'He makes me as surefooted as a deer, able to tread upon the heights' (3:19). These words are such a demonstration of trust, of confident expectation of good; they are witness to the transformation that Habakkuk has gone through. Habakkuk knows, in bone marrow depths, that *Yahweh* is with him, *Elohim* will strengthen him and *Adonai* will lead him into a future in which he will rescue joy from the jaws of despair. And this is God's desire for us; that we are not paralysed by fear, not crippled by the circumstances of our lives or our responses to them, but that we move on, move *through* those circumstances believing that there is so much more yet to be revealed, to us and in us. Liddell got it right I think when he wrote that, 'Our broken lives are not lost or useless. God's love is still working'.[19] And the strength of God's love is still at work for us today, whatever the nature of our brokenness, however lost or useless we might feel our lives to be. *Through* those very circumstances, the steady pulse of the love of God for us is beating with redemptive, transformative, action.

The Amplified Bible translates the last words sung by Habakkuk at the end of this little book in a particularly hope-filled, faith-packed, jubilant way:

> The Lord GOD is my Strength, my personal bravery, *and* my invincible army; He makes my feet like hinds' feet and will make me to walk [not to stand still in terror, but to walk] *and* make [spiritual] progress upon my high places [of trouble, suffering, or responsibility]!

And so there is hope – even among the ruins of our own dreams, through the grief of our own losses and the ache for what might never be in this life, what might never *again* be known, held, loved – that God is here, present, among our ruins, always, to the close of the age.

Practice: Brief prayer affirmations

Perhaps one of the most impressive aspects of Habakkuk's journey with God into the transformation which is so obvious to see in these last verses is that he didn't ignore the reality of where he was in his life. He faced it fully, wrestling through it with God until he got to that place where he could stand with God and face the future with hope and confidence, with courage and purpose.

Habakkuk's crescendo of 'even though's was followed by a cymbal-clashing 'yet'! That one word changed everything. A bit like adjusting the focus on a pair of binoculars until we see clearly, the word 'yet' is a word which helps to adjust the focus of the lens through which we view our circumstances. Habakkuk's 'yet' brought into clear focus what he knew to be true of God. He named the God of his experience, the God of his hope and those names became the platform on which he stood and from which he viewed the future and his place in it.

How would you name the God of your experience right now? Would your name be drawn from the richness of scripture – Rock, Shepherd, Door, Light, Life, Holy One, Strong Deliverer, Friend – or is there another name which more personally encapsulates your experience? Over the years, I have addressed God as 'my safest place', 'my hammock', 'the holder of my dreams' and 'my gentle nudger'. They might not be anyone else's choice, but those names were a true reflection of who I was experiencing God to be at that time.

So, pause here for a moment and answer the question, 'What is my name for God?'

Now, add a statement of truth or desire which expresses what you most need God to be or to do for you in your present circumstances.

- For the tax collector in Luke 18:9–14, his desire was, 'Be merciful to me, a sinner.'
- For the disciples, fearful and panicked in the midst of the storm, it was, 'Save us, we're drowning.'
- For Jairus, made desperate by his daughter's illness, it was, 'Please come, my daughter is dying.'
- For Bartimaeus, as he answered Jesus' question 'What do you want me to do for you?', his desire was, 'I want to see.'

How would you answer Jesus' question if he were to address you with these same words: 'What do you want me to do for you?'

Now, bring together your name for the God of your experience, and your answer to Jesus' question and write it out as a brief prayer. This is a prayer that you can pray throughout the day, a prayer packed with personal meaning and short enough to say in a moment. As we say this prayer, it becomes a conscious reminder that we are always in the welcoming presence of God, a deliberate acknowledgment of our need for him, an intentional act of remembrance. It is an affirmation of trust. It's also a way to fulfil Paul's injunction to 'never stop praying' (1 Thessalonians 5:17). I've found it helpful to adopt this prayer for a few weeks, or even months, until the circumstances that needed that prayer were changed, or until my perspective on them was altered.

A little while ago, my prayer was, 'O Peace of God, still me.' As I write, this is still my prayer as I face a number of transitions which have come all at the same time and my heart feels tossed about and a wee bit anxious. Throughout the day, I find myself praying this prayer; a shorthand for the desire and the need for a deep stillness that I have right now. As anxiety begins to rise, it is a prompt for this prayer.

As I look through my journal, I see other brief prayers which have been significant to me over these years, not just for my life, but also for the lives of those I love and care about: 'O Jesus, my beloved, may I be a joy to thee today.' (This was adapted from a prayer I found by Amy Carmichael and which I wrote on a Post-it note and stuck on my bathroom mirror and which stayed there for months.) 'Comforter God, hold her close' (for a friend going through a heart-breaking divorce). 'God of night, lighten his darkness' (prayed for a friend going through depression).

Whenever the Lord would bring one of these friends to mind, I would pray this simple brief prayer for them, knowing that these words held so much of my heart's desire for them, represented so much of my confidence in God to meet them in that place.

Perhaps your prayer might find its way on to a Post-it note, or into your journal, or as a banner on your computer or background on your phone. Wherever it ends up physically, the joy of these brief prayers is that they reach the heart of God, and open a space for his Spirit to enter with transforming power in our lives and the lives of those we love.

Chapter 8

Walking with the wounded

There are some problems that cannot be solved. They can only be lived through… There are times when friendship calls simply for a human presence, a listening ear and an understanding heart, so that soul can unburden to soul.
Rabbi Jonathan Sacks[20]

We know so little about Habakkuk. We don't know if he was married or if he had a family. We have a little inkling that he was part of the community based in the temple at Jerusalem, but we don't know if he had friends there, if there was anyone there who could walk with him through the distress of his days in ways that were strengthening and supportive and comforting. He seems to have walked this journey with God alone. But there is something in me which hopes that he had someone who would come alongside him at such a harrowing time in his life.

Walking with someone through the earthquakes, the blizzards, the ruined places of their lives is not for the faint-hearted – but it is for those whose hearts are so touched by God with the hurt and grief of others that it moves them into the storm, the desert places, the wilderness of another's life. It is for those who, in trusting dependence upon the Spirit of God, are willing to sit with the broken in the rubble of their dreams, the heartache of their losses and the devastation of their hope. To sit with them, and in that place to incarnate the love and the compassion and the hope of God.

I was very blessed to be gifted with many such brave-hearts during Jenny's treatment and death. God gave me men and women who, at different points on the journey, inspired courage and hope, who spoke the truth of God's word and reminded me of his character, who prayed with me and for me, and who sat with me in silence when the dreadful truth of the reality of Jenny's death was so crushingly heavy that words could not be spoken, would never have been a sufficient cradle to hold the pain.

Most of those God-sent ones were not counsellors or ministers or trained in some special way, but they did seem to share certain characteristics and skills which allowed them to come alongside in wisely comforting, nurturing and strengthening ways. No single person was able to give everything that I needed but, in the mercy of God, each person's gifting and contribution became part of a collage of healing which God put together so effectively. As we walk with the wounded, we may feel that our particular contribution seems so small and insignificant, but if that contribution is made in response to the leading of God's Spirit, then we can be sure that God will incorporate what we bring into the whole that is needed. As I've reflected on the qualities which made up my own particular collage of help, they seemed to mirror the quality of companionship which the newly resurrected Jesus offered two of his disciples on the Sunday after the crucifixion – a scene which Luke captures for us in his account recorded in Luke 24:13–35.

In this passage, Luke provides us with a case study of what walking with the wounded looks like in practice as he relates the account of Jesus coming alongside two of his disciples, bruised by the events they have witnessed over the weekend. They are bewildered and disoriented after their world has been turned upside down by Jesus' crucifixion and death. Luke picks up the story as they are heading home on the road that leads from Jerusalem to Emmaus.

Coming alongside

Luke tells us that 'Jesus himself suddenly came and began walking with them' (v. 15); and this is where this vital ministry begins for us too. Jesus drew alongside them, he came to the place and the space they were occupying at that moment, and he walked at their pace and in the direction they were going. Such a simple act, but such a challenging one to pull off well. Jesus didn't demand that those disciples be anywhere other than where they were at that time. He didn't demand that they speed up or slow down, take a different route or adopt a different attitude. He just came alongside and walked with them, and stopped with them as they shared their confusion and their hurt and their disappointed hopes. He was fully present to them, where they were, without any sense of needing to hurry them along to be anywhere else.

So often when we come alongside another at a broken time in their lives, we might feel that they should be moving faster, getting through this part of their journey more quickly. There can be a temptation to apply some kind of pre-stamped 'steps to healing' template, or a set timetable for recovery or 'moving on', which we might feel is more appropriate or helpful for where they are. We might be tempted to nudge them prematurely into a different space – emotionally or relationally or spiritually – than they are ready to occupy. Sometimes we want to ease them out of their pain rather than stand with them in it. And when we do this, we violate the sometimes slow healing of the work of God in a person's life and we dishonour their unique journey.

Whatever the nature of the ruined place in our lives, that ruin will be accompanied by significant loss. And losses need to be grieved over in whatever manner and through whatever time is needed. We can damage the healing process by suggesting that a person has had long enough to grieve, or that they should 'be over it' by now. When we do this, we are adding to a burden which is already heavy to bear. My experience is that processing loss takes however long it takes and, although there may be common features, the timing of a person's healing through grief, the time it takes to forgive or to let go of fear or anger or bitterness, is unique to that individual. 'Models' of recovery or healing, however helpful, need to be so cautiously applied.

An open space

The next thing Jesus does is to make an observation and then to ask some questions. He effectively said, 'You look sad, what's going on? Tell me more.' He could so easily have said, 'Hey guys, don't be so down – look, it's me!' But he didn't. He knew that these two disciples needed the opportunity to articulate in their own words what was going on inside of them. His observation was discerning; his questions were an invitation to make whatever response they needed to make at that time. His questions gave them an open, safe space to express the broken hopes and the dashed expectations which were gripping their hearts: 'We *had hoped* he was the Messiah who had come to rescue Israel' (v. 21), they tell him, and in that one sentence is basketed all of their wrecked dreams and shattered promises.

And this again is a concrete action we can take as we come alongside another; we can create a safe space in which the words that need to be said can be said without fear or reproach. We do this by giving time to the person, as much time as is needed, for them to bring into the open the fears, the anxieties, the anger, the doubt, the grief – whatever it is that needs to be expressed. In the context of our conversation, we become a safe non-judgemental presence for a person by not judging what we are hearing either with a word or a look, by not interrupting, by not changing the course in which the conversation is moving, by trusting that the Holy Spirit is well used to the time it takes for us to reach and to express our reality and he invites us as listeners to walk at his non-rushed pace.

Open the word

Jesus' next words may not seem to be a helpful response for us to follow: 'You foolish people!' he exclaims. To our 21st-century ears, this is an insensitive insult, but in the context in which Jesus spoke these words, these first-century disciples would have interpreted the comment in the context of the next phrase, 'You find it so hard to believe all that the prophets wrote in the Scriptures.' The book of Proverbs seems to equate 'foolishness' with a slowness to believe God's word and wisdom. This was not an insult to their intelligence; this was Jesus' drawing their attention to their lack of belief in the word of God through a phrase which would immediately connect with their understanding of what the scriptures considered wise, and what foolish.

Having drawn their attention to their lack of understanding, Jesus didn't leave them there, but engaged them in an Old Testament Bible study through 'all the Scriptures… concerning himself'. His intent seems to be to help them gain a new perspective on who he was. He knew that the disciples' perspective was limited to certain aspects of how the Messiah would appear and how he would accomplish his purpose; they needed a much broader, richer perspective, and Jesus took them to the scriptures to do that. As a result, hope was ignited and their 'hearts burned within them'. Jesus brought new hope and courage in a seemingly hopeless situation. They were excited and energised as they heard the word of God. Jesus didn't focus on the problem of dashed expectations and disappointment and try and fix that with some sound advice. Not now. Their biggest need at this time was a deeper understanding of who he was, and so he drew them to the word of God, and applied that word specifically and skilfully to their need.

I was so very blessed to receive such a restorative and reorienting ministry from wise and caring friends, who walked with me through my own wounded days. Most times, when we are bewildered or distressed or in pain, we don't need a theological explanation of suffering; we need to be reminded that we are still cared for by the God who understands our suffering so very well and who is present with us in it. We need to be gently drawn to passages of scripture which will build hope and confidence in God, and which will turn us from fear and despair to the sustaining truths of God's character and purposes revealed in his word.

Perhaps the most effective use of the scriptures at this time is when they are introduced with the words, 'When I was going through _____, this verse really spoke to me; I don't know if it will help you…' or 'I read this recently and I'm praying it for you…' Scriptures which come from the integrity of our lived experience with God, especially in our own tough times, can sometimes touch the tender place in another person's life more surely than a random verse on the character of God, no matter how well-intentioned. We don't need to be Bible scholars or counsellors to share God's word in this way, but we do need to be wise and prayerful and sensitive to the Holy Spirit, the wisest counsellor of all, to lead us in our sharing.

On their terms

After this Bible study, Jesus is invited to spend longer with these two disciples. The initiative had been taken by Jesus, but now as he is preparing to leave them, they invite him to come home with them and to eat with them, which in Jewish culture at that time was a gesture of friendship, an invitation to a more intimate fellowship. And Jesus accepted their invitation; he did go to their home, he did sit at the table with them – and as soon as they recognised him, he disappeared!

What is going on in this strange moment that could possibly be helpful to us? Perhaps a couple of practical applications might be helpful for us to consider here: the first is the willingness to accept the invitation to enter more deeply into another person's world. Secondly, we should have the wisdom to know when it would be appropriate to withdraw from that world and to leave the person to reflect more personally on the experience that has been shared.

In many ways, Luke has presented us with a masterclass on companioning and soul care here, but after these broad-brush strokes, there may be further elements to look at in more detail which would be helpful for our own ministry of walking with the wounded.

Don't assume

From Jesus' opening words we learn something so obvious, but which we can sometimes forget in our eagerness to help, and that is our need to be careful not to assume we already know how this person is feeling or thinking about the situation they are in. The book of Proverbs wisely reminds us that 'each heart knows its own bitterness' (14:10). However many common elements there may be with similar stories we may have heard, *this* story and *this* person's experience is individual and unique.

The people who helped me the most when walking with me through my own wounded experience were those who said, 'I can't imagine what you are going through right now.' The less helpful were those who confidently assured me that they knew just what I was going through because… and then told me a story from their own experience. We can be empathetic with the person going through their experience without having to match that experience with one of our own. We can draw from the emotions which our own experience evoked in us and use that as a platform from which to empathise – but the experience itself doesn't necessarily need to be shared, at least in the early days of the journey. There may be times when what we hear has no point of contact with our own experience and at such times we may actually need to admit that we don't know what to say or do, but we are here. We are present. And it is enough.

Listen well

Jesus was a good listener. Before he spoke a word of hope or encouragement or wisdom, he listened well and long as they poured out their hearts to him. These disciples were trying to process so much and, in his listening, Jesus created the space that was needed for this coming to terms with reality. 'Being taken seriously and listened to are among the most healing realities we can offer individuals,' writes Marjorie Thompson in her book on encouragement.[21]

For us, too, attentive listening is a means by which we can enter into the reality of the person we are coming alongside. Very rarely are words better than silence when we are walking with the wounded. Good listening, according to Henry Nouwen, is an act of spiritual hospitality.[22] Whether we can identify with someone or not, whether we can empathise or not, we need to understand that we are not called or required to fix the hurt or the sadness or the pain. It's not our job to make it go away. We can't. We are not responsible for the healing or the changes that may need to occur, but we can be responsive to the Holy Spirit as he leads us in our listening. Rabbi Jonathan Sacks has written that, 'There are some problems that cannot be solved. They can only be lived through… There are times when friendship calls simply for a human presence, a listening ear and an understanding heart, so that soul can unburden to soul.'[23]

And this is what Jesus has provided for here: an opportunity for soul to unburden to soul. In my own training as a counsellor and spiritual director, one of the most helpful questions I learned to ask when listening was, 'Can you tell me more about that?' Such a simple question, but so wonderfully reassuring for the person who is being listened to because it affirms that they are being heard, that what they say is being taken seriously and that there is a real desire on our part to understand them. I have never had any person, in my many years of asking this question, not answer it. So often people begin to tell us their story and then they stop. And if we jump in with our response too quickly, we may rob them of the chance to continue. Very often the stopping is a test: 'Are you with me? Are you truly listening or are you just waiting for a chance to tell me what you think?' Our silent affirmation, a nod of the head, an affirming 'hmm', our restful, non-judgemental presence as we wait for what comes next gives permission and confidence for the person to carry on speaking.

Listening is an art, a discipline, a skill, a gift wrapped in quiet presence. It is a characteristic of God, the great listener of our inarticulate souls, whose patient listening enables us to find the words to express what is going on inside. Good listening is always a godly act, an incarnation of the heart of God in our conversations.

Encourage

After their encounter with Jesus, the disciples exclaimed, 'Didn't our hearts burn within us?' (Luke 24:32). This little phrase is a snapshot of encouragement. The true meaning of the word 'encourage' is to put the heart back into a person. So often the person we are drawing alongside, like these disciples on the Emmaus road, has lost heart, has lost hope, has lost the courage to go on, has lost what it takes to believe God for one more time. One of the gifts we can bring at such a time is encouragement; but not the 'Don't worry, be happy' kind of false encouragement which God actually condemns. Through the prophet Jeremiah, God accuses the false prophets of not honouring the seriousness of the wounds of his people. God states, 'My people are broken – shattered! – and they put on Band-Aids, saying, "It's not so bad. You'll be just fine"' (Jeremiah 6:14, *The Message*). Nothing is healed when the wound, the brokenness, the loss, is not honoured, when it is dismissed so lightly.

The encouragement that heals and brings new hope doesn't flinch from the reality that is present, but it brings the truth of the word of God into that present and incarnates that truth through our presence. Over and over again in my journal, I recorded the scriptures which people passed on to me. So many of them were like lifebuoys which kept me afloat till I could stand on firm land again. The word of God, skilfully and lovingly offered, is truly a source of hope and encouragement and healing, and we need to be prepared to use it well, and so very wisely and prayerfully as we draw alongside others.

Pray

Such a simple act, such a simple expression of loving care, but such a significant ministry in a person's life at this time. We can pray for the person, for their emotional, physical and spiritual well-being. We can ask God to give us insight into how to pray specifically for them and trust that he will give us what is on his heart for us to pray. And perhaps, on occasion, we can tell them that we are praying and what we are praying. So many times, loving friends would send me a brief text to tell me what they were praying for me. I still have on my phone some of the texts that my friend Rosemary has sent me over the years in which she has told me specifically what she is praying for me – what she is trusting God for me. There may be times when we really don't know what to pray for a person and, at those times, I've found it helpful to turn to the scriptures.

Praying the prayers of Paul is a helpful beginning for us. Whether writing to a beleaguered church or an unsteady group, he prays that they would be strengthened in their inner being so that they would discern God's will for them in this time. He prays they would experience the full dimensions of God's love. He prays that their faith would hold and be strong. He prays that they would know that they were cared for by God and that God had purposes for their lives. We can pray these same requests for the wounded ones we walk with. And we can pray *with* them too. Sometimes we may ask someone if we can pray with them, and the answer is no. When this happens, we can assure them that we will be praying for them even if we are not praying with them. There are times when a person is so bruised that even to be prayed with is more than they can handle. But to know that they are prayed for can be strengthening and an assurance that God has been invited to take his place in this part of their lives and that he cares deeply about what is happening.

Take the initiative

Being in a wounded place can leave a person feeling lonely, isolated, vulnerable. And because of the deep weariness that often accompanies such a time, there can be a sense that there just isn't the energy to articulate what is needed, what is wanted. This is why it's important when walking with the wounded for us to take the initiative with them. Very often because we don't know what to say or do, we don't say or do anything. During my own weary time, I experienced God's movement toward me through the kindness of people like my friend Rachel who, with her hands full with small children somehow found the time to cook meals for my freezer. She never asked what she could do; she just did it and turned up with the food. We can take the initiative to communicate, to be in touch; not necessarily by phone, which demands a response, but a quick text message, an email, a card. Another Rachael, my spiritual director, was so good at doing this. Every now and then she would send a little card, a beautiful picture, with just a few words of encouragement or comfort on the back. I still have one of those cards in my purse today; it is a prayer by Kierkegaard, 'My Lord God, give me once more the courage to hope.'[24] I prayed and prayed and prayed that prayer. Every time I opened my purse – there it was and on the back in Rachael's beautiful calligraphy, brief words of love and support. It doesn't take much to take the initiative, but it does take time and thought and effort. But it is so worth it.

Over the course of Jenny's cancer treatment and her death, I experienced so many varied forms of creative initiative. One of my friends paid for me to have a cleaner for a little while; some of my colleagues helped by picking up on some of the academic load I was carrying at that time, lifting the administrative load that comes with university level teaching; another dear friend invited me to her home for the weekend and treated me so very kindly in every single way from candles in my room to bubbles in my bath, to good food and gentle conversation. Nothing was demanded of me; I only needed to show up. She recognised my need for rest, for beauty, for unforced, non-demanding presence – and she gave it generously. As we are sensitive to the person and sensitive to the nudgings of the Holy Spirit, we will find that there are so many different ways of taking the initiative. As we ask gentle questions about rest and sleep, about diet and exercise, we may be able to draw attention to the practical needs of body and soul. Often people need prompting to pay attention and to care for their needs at this time; our questions can provide such prompting.

Finally, so often as we walk with another in the harder darker parts of their journey, we might find ourselves taking on more than we should, taking on more responsibility and shouldering more of the burden for their lives than is appropriate. If we are to be present with another in the ways described above, then we need also to be present to God in ways that are refreshing for our own souls; ways which help us keep a healthy distance from being entangled in what we are hearing, and which give us space and time to process what we are hearing.

There are times when I find myself walking with someone in paths that become very challenging for my own soul. I listen to such distress, and sometimes am invited to speak into situations for which I feel totally inadequate. It is in these times that I will ask the person I'm companioning for permission to share their story anonymously with someone else for prayer and counsel. There are times when we need to recognise that as much as we care for a person and want to be available to help, we do not have the capacity or the resources that are necessary for this particular need.

Through the experiences of these past years, I've come to believe that walking with the wounded, being present with them as they stand in the ruins of their lives, is probably one of the most challenging, costly, but privileged ministries we may ever have in a person's life as we incarnate the love and the care and the kind wisdom of God in that hurting place.

Habakkuk wrestled and struggled, cried and grieved, and eventually, true to his name, embraced God and his purposes with joy and hopefulness. The integrity of his journey with God made him such a gift of a companion on my own journey through the ruins left by Jenny's cancer and death. Looking back, I'm profoundly grateful for the ways in which walking with Habakkuk has brought healing to my soul, a richer understanding of the person and the purposes of God, and perhaps more than anything, a deepened, confident assurance that Emmanuel, God with us, will continue to be with me, walk with me, stay with me through whatever lies ahead. And in the depth of that truth lies hope and joy and the wonder of transformation… Even though… even here.

Postscript

Even though… even here… Emmanuel

On the very day when I submitted the manuscript for this book, I was diagnosed with breast cancer. It felt as though a journey which had been initiated by Jenny's cancer was coming full circle, and home again to those early morning wake-up words: 'Even though… even here… Emmanuel.' The truths that were explored through the writing of the book have been even more richly experienced over these months since my diagnosis. God's presence and God's peace have been sustaining realities even in the midst of the disappointment of a second surgery and the unwelcomed side effects of treatment. In some ways, I sense a new kinship with Habakkuk as I've realised in a fresh way that *even though* cancer has entered into my life as an uninvited guest, *yet* I can live with passion and with purpose the days that God has gifted to me, knowing that my life is held in the kindest and strongest hands, cradled gently in the mystery of his goodness and in the wisdom of his purposes.

It is a good place to be.

Notes

1 Eric Liddell, *Disciplines of the Christian Life* (SPCK, 2009), p. 122.
2 Frederick Buechner, *Beyond Words: Daily readings in the ABCs of faith* (HarperSanFrancisco, 2004), p. 109.
3 Eugene Peterson, 'Introduction to Habakkuk' in Tʜᴇ Mᴇssᴀɢᴇ (Navpress, 2009), p. 1272.
4 Richard Rohr, 'Don't miss the second half', *U.S. Catholic Magazine*, 70.8 (August, 2005), pp. 24–28.
5 Walter Brueggemann, *Spirituality of the Psalms* (Fortress Press, 2002).
6 Marjorie J. Thompson, *The Gift of Encouragement: Restoring heart to those who have lost it* (Abingdon Press, 2013 – Kindle edition).
7 Taken from *When Life Takes What Matters* © 1993 by Susan Lenzkes. Used by permission of Discovery House Publishers, Box 3566, Grand Rapids MI 4950l. All rights reserved.
8 C.S. Lewis, *Letters to Malcolm* (Harvest Books, 2002), p. 20.
9 Ken Gire, *Life as We Would Want It… Life as We Are Given It* (Nelson Bibles, 2007), pp. 91, 93.
10 Marjorie J. Thompson, *Soul Feast* (Westminster John Knox Press, 2005), p. 39.
11 Peterson, 'Introduction to Habakkuk', p. 1272, quoted in Stephen W. Smith, *The Lazarus Life* (David C. Cook, 2009), p. 41.
12 Ephesians 1:4–5.
13 Nicholas P. Wolterstorff, *Lament for a Son* (Eerdmans, 1996), p. 81.
14 George Everett Ross, quoted in Philip Yancey, *Reaching for the Invisible God: What can we expect to find* (Zondervan, 2002), pp. 52–53.
15 Adele Ahlberg Calhoun, *Invitations from God* (IVP, 2011), p. 145.
16 Liddell, *Disciplines of the Christian Life*, p. 122.
17 Habakkuk 3:17–19, my paraphrase.
18 Joan Chittister, *Scarred by Struggle, Transformed by Hope* (Eerdmans, 2003), p. 107.
19 Liddell, *Disciplines of the Christian Life*, p. 122.
20 Rabbi Jonathan Sacks, 'Listening is the greatest gift we can give our troubled souls', *The Times* (14 December 2002).
21 Thompson, *The Gift of Encouragement*.
22 Henri Nouwen, *Bread for the Journey* (HarperOne, 2006), p. 80.
23 Sacks, 'Listening is the greatest gift'.
24 Alexander Dru (ed.), *The Soul of Kierkegaard: Selections from his journals* (Dover Publications, Inc., 2003), p. 68.

DEEP CALLS
TO DEEP
SPIRITUAL FORMATION
IN THE HARD PLACES
OF LIFE
TONY
HORSFALL

INCLUDES GROUP MATERIAL

Is there a positive purpose to suffering? How many times have you heard
that question? And how many times have you felt that the answers are too
simple – perhaps even naive? But what if suffering actually has a positive
purpose? What if suffering is the only state in which humans stand empty
enough before God to learn and grow? Popular author and retreat leader
Tony Horsfall turns his attention to the raw pain and honesty of suffering
found in the Psalms of Lament, psalms that show the psalmist daring to
be real and straight with God.

Deep Calls to Deep
Spiritual formation in the hard places of life
Tony Horsfall
978 1 84101 731 0 £7.99

brfonline.org.uk

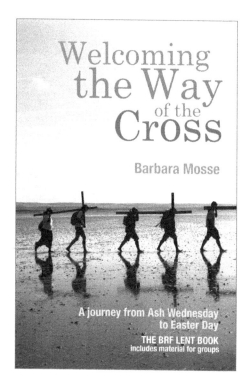

Do you have concerns, uncertainty or even fear about what it means to deny self and follow Jesus? Retreat leader and spirituality tutor Barbara Mosse suggests such fears are based on misunderstanding. Following Jesus should not be a journey of fear but one of welcome, helping you find within a deep sense of hospitality for God, your fellow human beings and your own inner shadow side. This is the heart of the gospel.

Welcoming the Way of the Cross
A journey from Ash Wednesday to Easter Day
Barbara Mosse
978 0 85746 180 3 £7.99

brfonline.org.uk

Facing Death

Rachel Boulding

This book of 18 undated reflections draws comfort and encouragement from the Bible and from the author's own experience for those going through life-limiting illness and for their family and carers. With moving vulnerability and without denying the difficult reality of the situation, Rachel Boulding suggests a way to confront terminal illness with faith and hope in a loving God.

Facing Death
Rachel Boulding
978 0 85746 564 1 £3.99

brfonline.org.uk

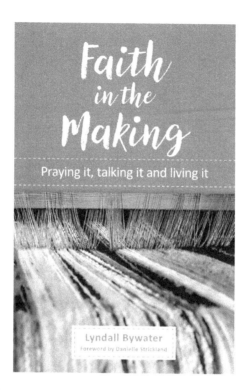

If 'faith is being sure of what we hope for and certain of what we do not see', what does that look like in practice today? In a world that is largely unsure and uncertain, how do we gain our confidence? *Faith in the Making* recognises the problem and seeks the answer in the list of faithful heroes found in Hebrews 11. This accessible devotional resource will inspire individuals and groups to live more confidently for God in today's world. Heroic faith is far more attainable than we often think!

Faith in the Making
Praying it, talking it and living it
Lyndall Bywater
978 0 85746 555 9 £7.99

brfonline.org.uk

Transforming
lives and communities

Christian growth and understanding of the Bible

Resourcing individuals, groups and leaders in churches for their own spiritual journey and for their ministry

Church outreach in the local community

Offering three programmes that churches are embracing to great effect as they seek to engage with their local communities and transform lives

Teaching Christianity in primary schools

Working with children and teachers to explore Christianity creatively and confidently

Children's and family ministry

Working with churches and families to explore Christianity creatively and bring the Bible alive

Visit **brf.org.uk** for more information on BRF's work

brf.org.uk